LEARNING ABC'S WORKBOOK

Letter tracing and activities to help your child learn the alphabet

Autumn McKay

> Find me on Instagram!
> @BestMomIdeas

Learning ABC's Workbook: Print by Autumn McKay
Published by Creative Ideas Publishing

www.BestMomIdeas.com

© 2019 Autumn McKay

All rights reserved. No portion of this book may be reproduced in any form without permission from the author, except as permitted by U.S. copyright law.

For permissions contact:
Permissions@BestMomIdeas.com

ISBN: 9781952016097

Table of Contents

Introduction vi

A
    Coloring 1
    Activity 2
    Uppercase Tracing 3
    Lowercase Tracing 4

B
    Coloring 5
    Activity 6
    Uppercase Tracing 7
    Lowercase Tracing 8

C
    Coloring 9
    Activity 11
    Uppercase Tracing 13
    Lowercase Tracing 14

D
    Coloring 15
    Activity 16
    Uppercase Tracing 17
    Lowercase Tracing 18

E
    Coloring 19
    Activity 20
    Uppercase Tracing 21
    Lowercase Tracing 22

F
    Coloring 23
    Activity 24

Uppercase Tracing 25
Lowercase Tracing 26

G
Coloring 27
Activity 28
Uppercase Tracing 29
Lowercase Tracing 30

H
Coloring 31
Activity 32
Uppercase Tracing 33
Lowercase Tracing 34

I
Coloring 35
Activity 37
Uppercase Tracing 39
Lowercase Tracing 40

J
Coloring 41
Activity 42
Uppercase Tracing 43
Lowercase Tracing 44

K
Coloring 45
Activity 46
Uppercase Tracing 47
Lowercase Tracing 48

L
Coloring 49
Activity 50
Uppercase Tracing 51
Lowercase Tracing 52

M
Coloring 53
Activity 54
Uppercase Tracing 55
Lowercase Tracing 56

N
Coloring 57
Activity 58
Uppercase Tracing 59
Lowercase Tracing 60

O
Coloring 61
Activity 62
Uppercase Tracing 63
Lowercase Tracing 64

P
Coloring 65
Activity 67
Uppercase Tracing 69
Lowercase Tracing 70

Q
Coloring 71
Activity 72
Uppercase Tracing 73
Lowercase Tracing 74

R
Coloring 75
Activity 76
Uppercase Tracing 77
Lowercase Tracing 78

S
- Coloring 79
- Activity 80
- Uppercase Tracing 81
- Lowercase Tracing 82

T
- Coloring 83
- Activity 84
- Uppercase Tracing 85
- Lowercase Tracing 86

U
- Coloring 87
- Activity 88
- Uppercase Tracing 89
- Lowercase Tracing 90

V
- Coloring 91
- Activity 93
- Uppercase Tracing 95
- Lowercase Tracing 96

W
- Coloring 97
- Activity 98
- Uppercase Tracing 99
- Lowercase Tracing 100

X
- Coloring 101
- Activity 102
- Uppercase Tracing 103
- Lowercase Tracing 104

Y
- Coloring 105
- Activity 106
- Uppercase Tracing 107
- Lowercase Tracing 108

Z
- Coloring 109
- Activity 110
- Uppercase Tracing 111
- Lowercase Tracing 112

Alphabet Practice 113
Tracing Practice 117

INTRODUCTION FOR LEARNING ABC's WORKBOOK: PRINT

I'm going to use the pronoun he throughout the introduction, but please know I thought of your sweet little girl too as I created this book.

I'm so glad to be a part of your little one's journey to learn ABC's! It is my hope that you and your child have fun as he learns each letter. In this workbook you will find a coloring page with the letter and picture, an activity page to practice identifying the letter, and two tracing pages—one for the uppercase letter and one for the lowercase letter. There is also a review activity and extra tracing pages located at the end of the book.

Learning ABC's is an important step in learning to read. A child who can name all the letters in the alphabet will be equipped with an important foundation toward recognizing sounds and printed words. Having mastery of letter names can make learning letter sounds easier for children because the sounds of many letter names are closely related to the letter sounds.

Here are a few tips and suggestions I recommend for using this book:

- First and foremost, have fun with your child as he is learning ABC's! The objective of this book is to help your child learn his ABC's, but also to build his confidence as he is learning new information and skills.

- Sit with your child as he is working through the workbook.

    - **ABC Coloring Page**: Point to the letter on the page, say it out loud to your child, and ask him to repeat the letter back to you. Say the letter sound to your child, and ask him to repeat it back to you. Explain that the picture starts with the letter.

    - **ABC Activity Page**: Identify the letter you are working on by telling him the letter name and letter sound. Help guide your child through the activity.

    - **Tracing Pages**: Instruct your child where to place the pencil, and how to follow the dotted line to each shape. Cheer him on as he practices tracing the dotted letters and especially as he writes the upper and lowercase letters on his own. You can, constructively, correct tracing techniques as needed.

- You are welcome to choose the order in which you would like to complete the book. I do suggest starting with the letters your child already knows or letters in his name.

- As you and your child are learning new letters, it's always fun to look for those letters in the world around you. Point out the letters on signs, on stores, on toys, or in books. This will help your child become more familiar with the letter and letter sound.

- When your child completes the workbook feel free to use the digital code in the back of the book to print the graduation certificate to celebrate your child's accomplishment.

Most importantly, let your child have fun and enjoy the learning process!

Color the picture.

Help the **astronaut** find his way to the **apple** tree.

Start on the ●. Follow the dotted line up to the ■ and down to the ▲. Place your pencil on the ♦. Trace across to the ♥.

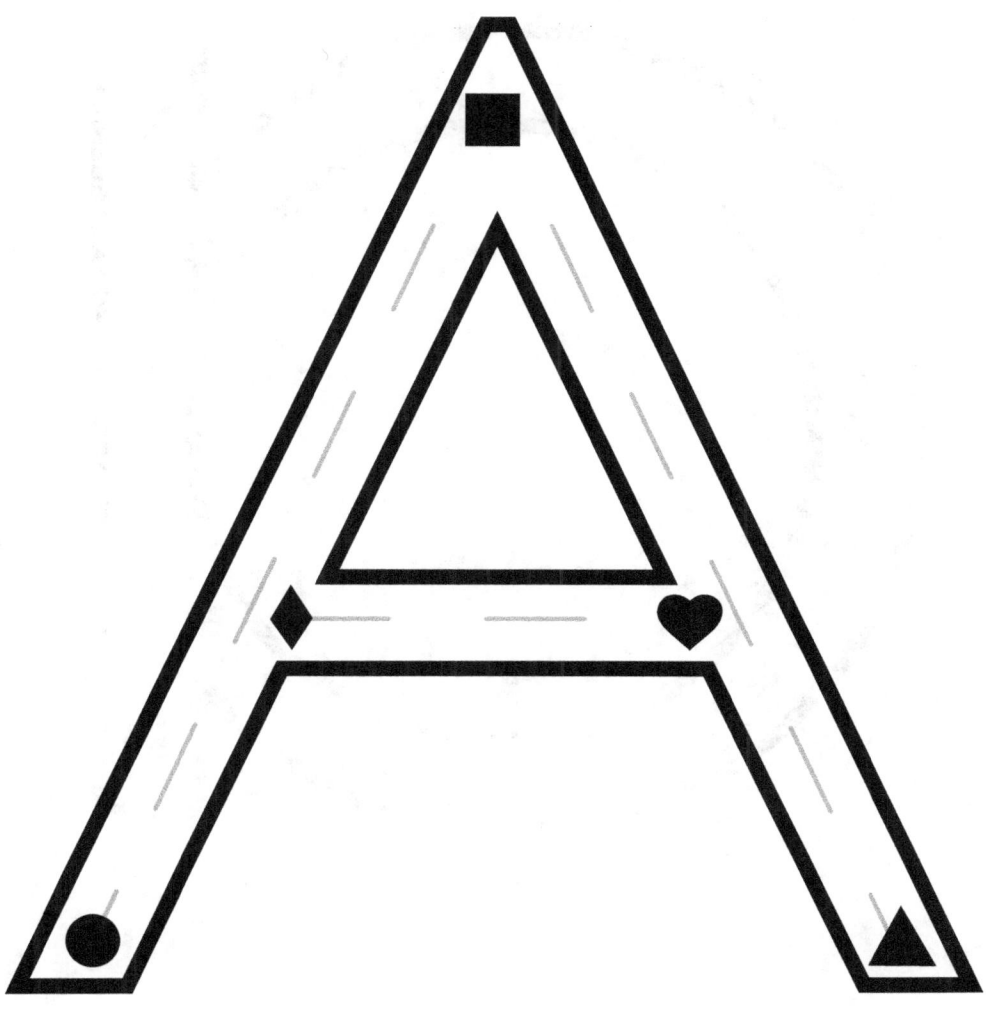

Practice tracing the uppercase A.

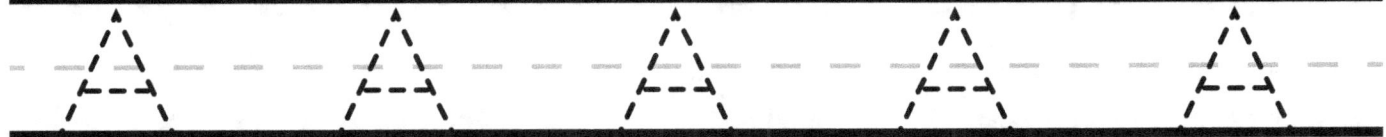

Now, try writing an uppercase A on your own.

Start on the ●. Follow the dotted line around to the ■. Place your pencil on the ▲. Trace down to the ◆.

Practice tracing the lowercase a.

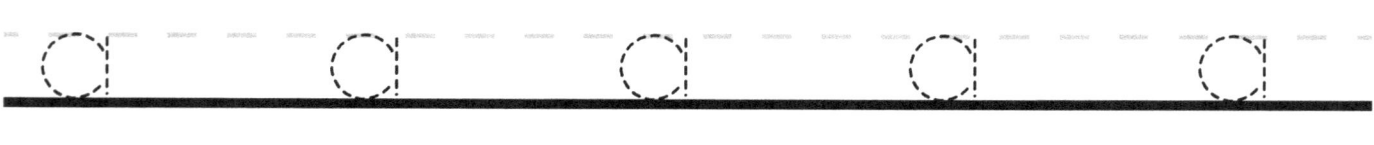

Now, try writing a lowercase a on your own.

Color the picture.

B

b

Place a sticker in each circle to form the letter B.

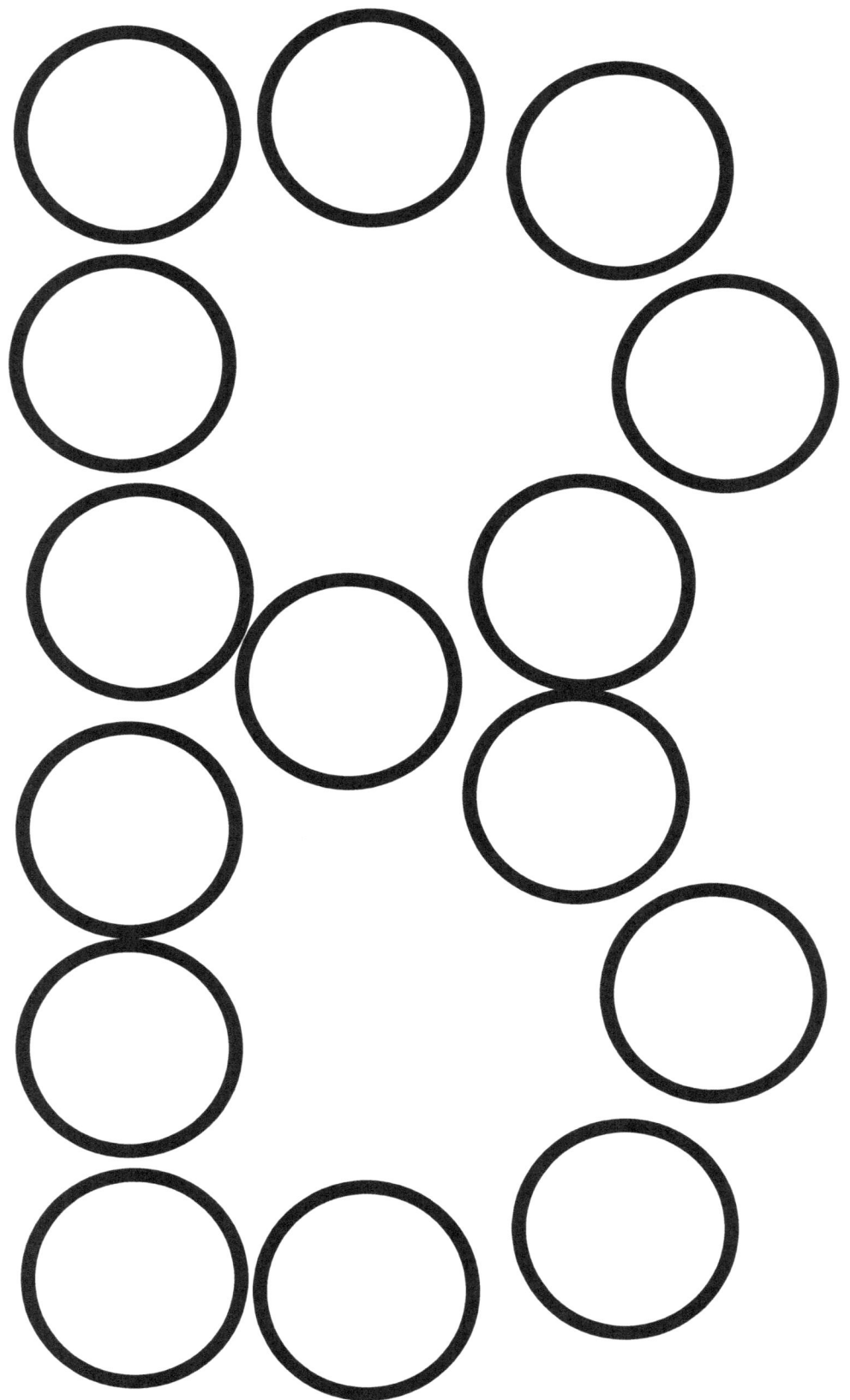

Start on the ● and trace the dotted line down to the ■. Place your pencil on the ▲, trace around to the ♦ and around the the ♥.

Practice tracing the uppercase B.

Now, try writing an uppercase B on your own.

Place your pencil on the ●. Follow the dotted line down to the ■. Place your pencil on the ▲, and follow the dotted line around the the ◆.

Practice tracing the lowercase b.

Now, try writing a lowercase b on your own.

Color the picture.

Cut out the letter C.

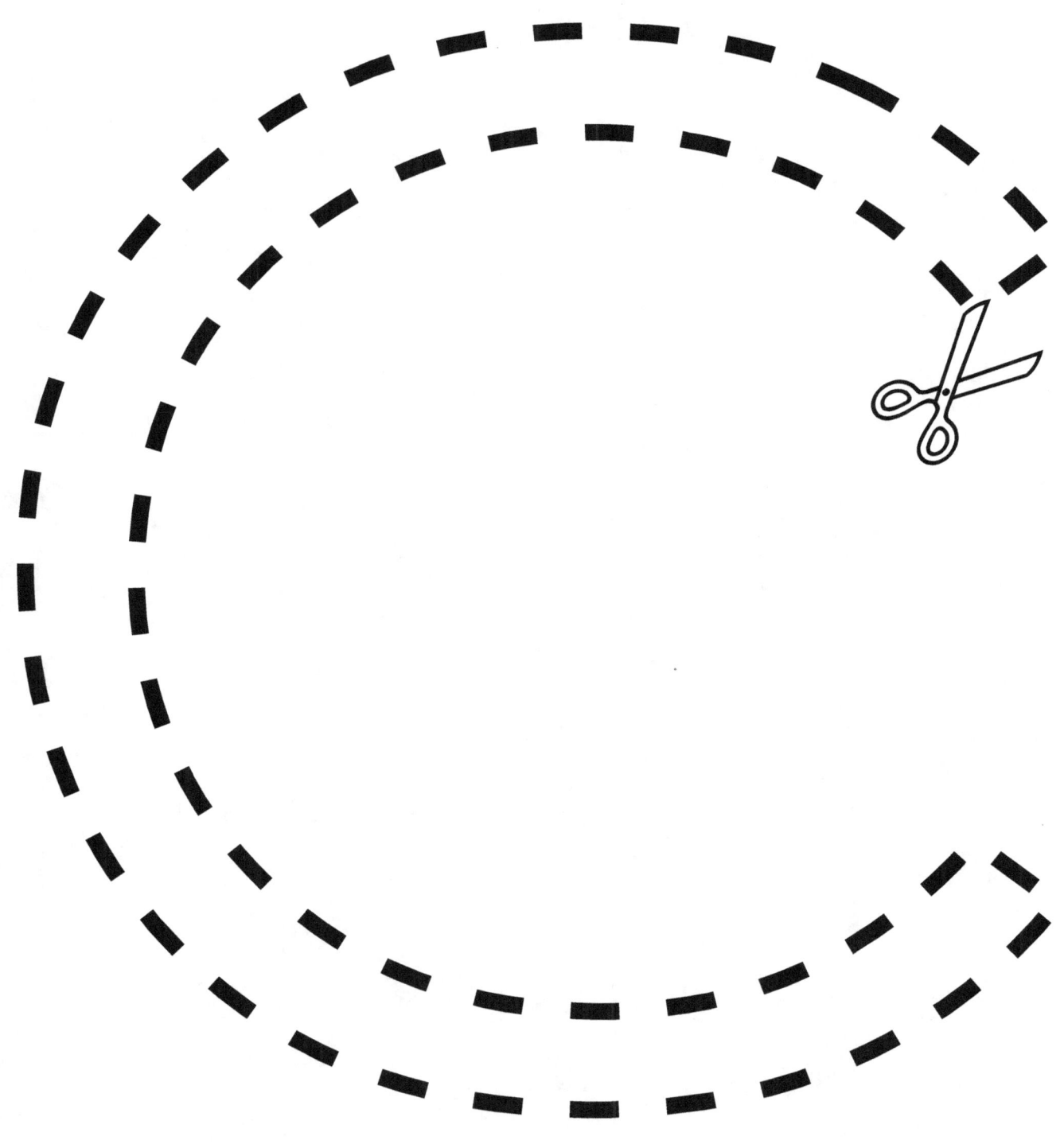

Left blank for cutting purposes.

Start at the ●. Trace around to the ■.

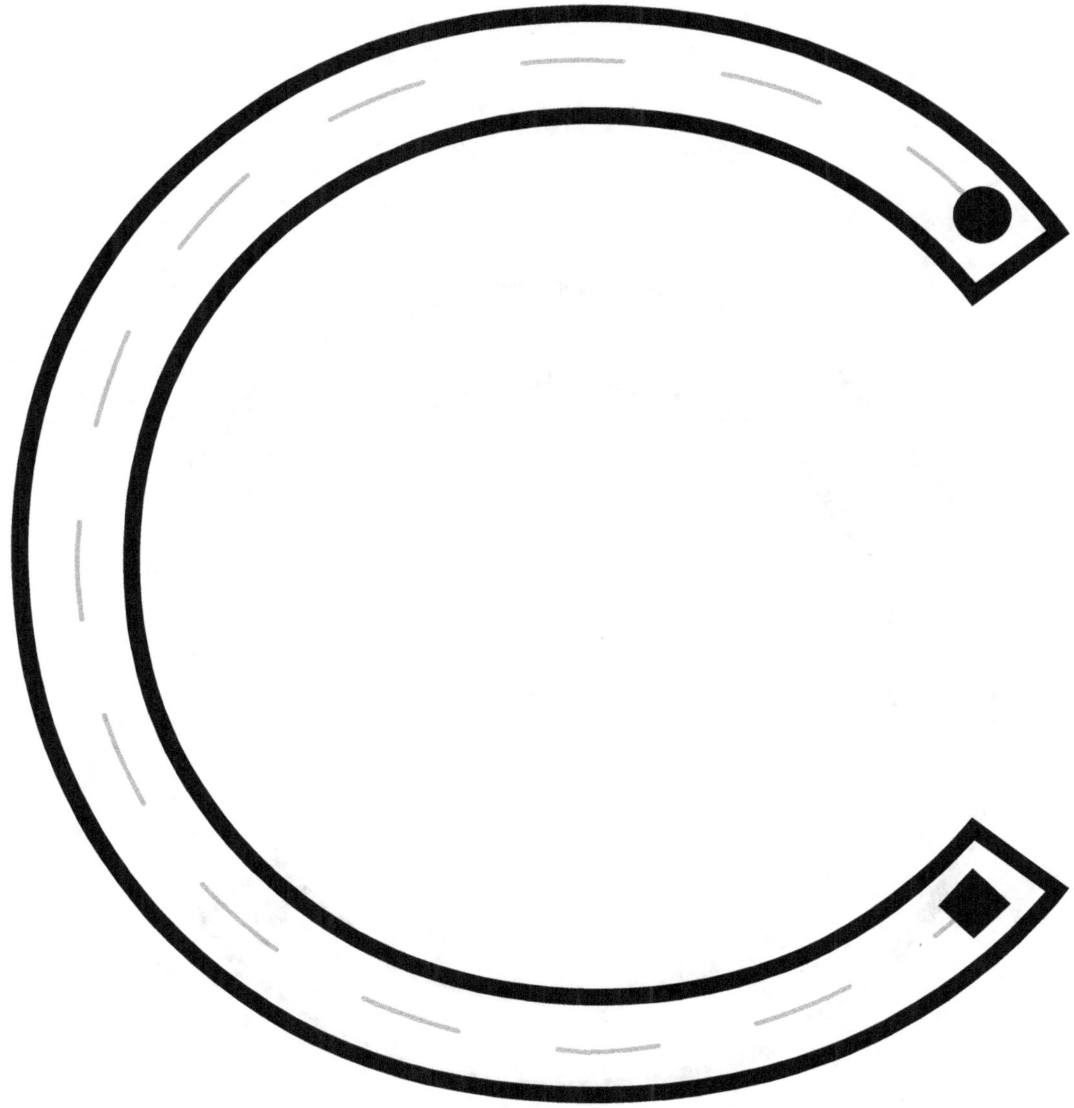

Practice tracing the uppercase C.

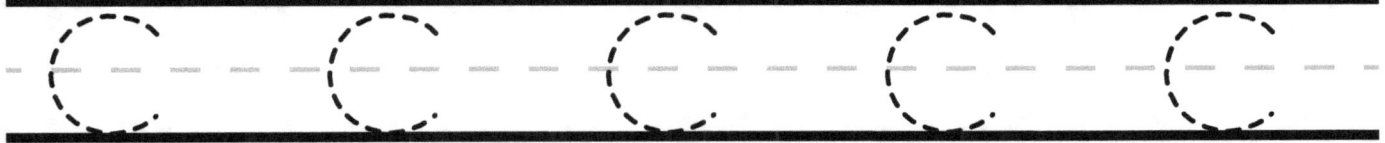

Now, try writing an uppercase C on your own.

Start at the ●. Trace around to the ■.

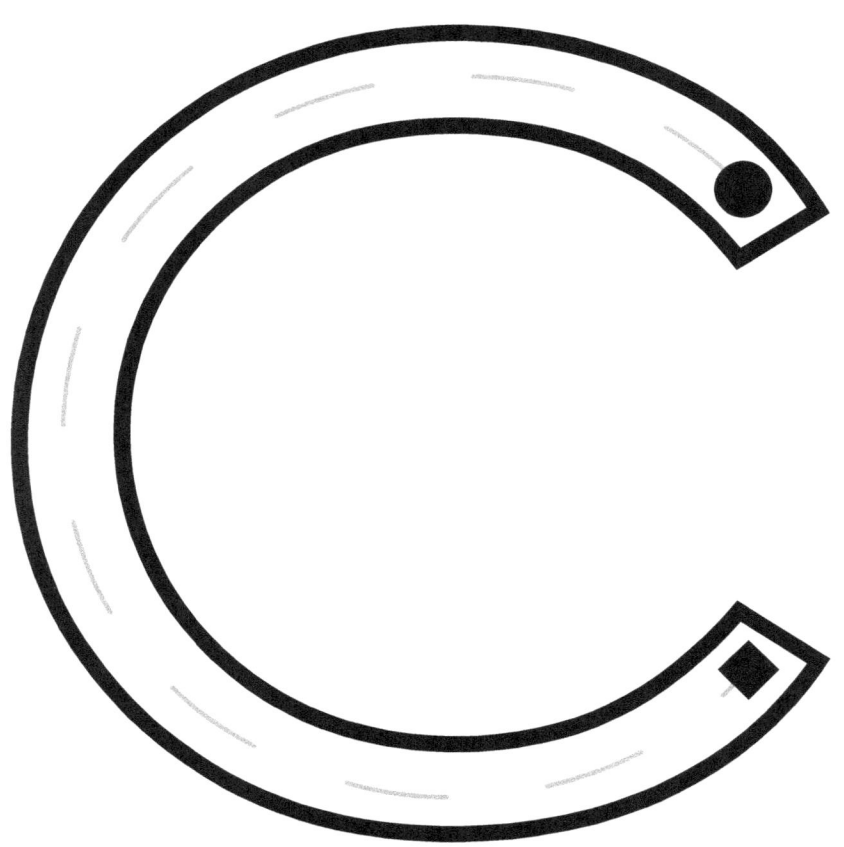

Practice tracing the lowercase c.

Now, try writing a lowercase c on your own.

Color the picture.

Find the hidden picture by coloring all of the uppercase D's and lowercase d's in the picture.

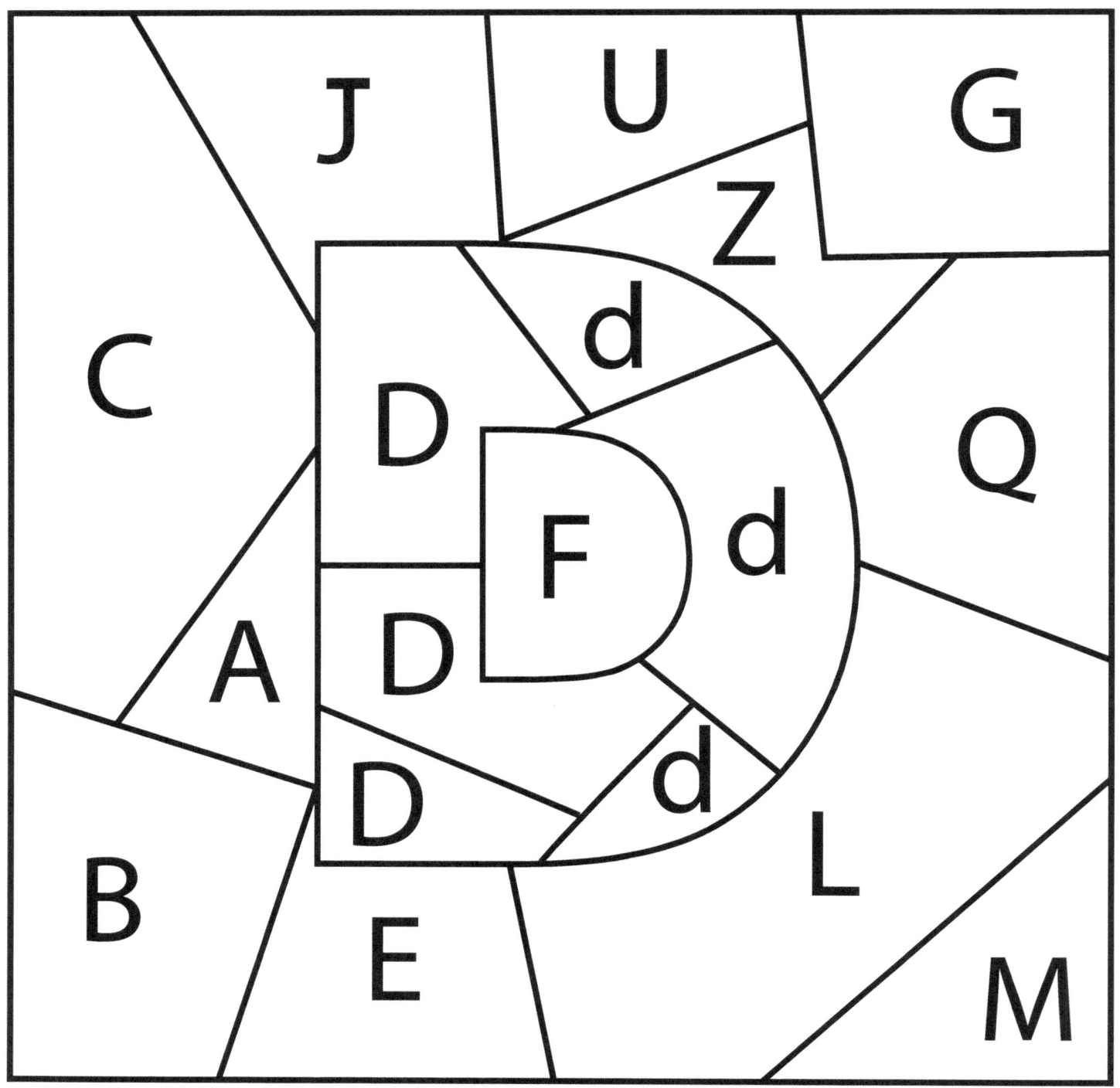

Start at the ●. Trace down to the ■. Place your pencil on the ▲, and follow the dotted line around to the ◆.

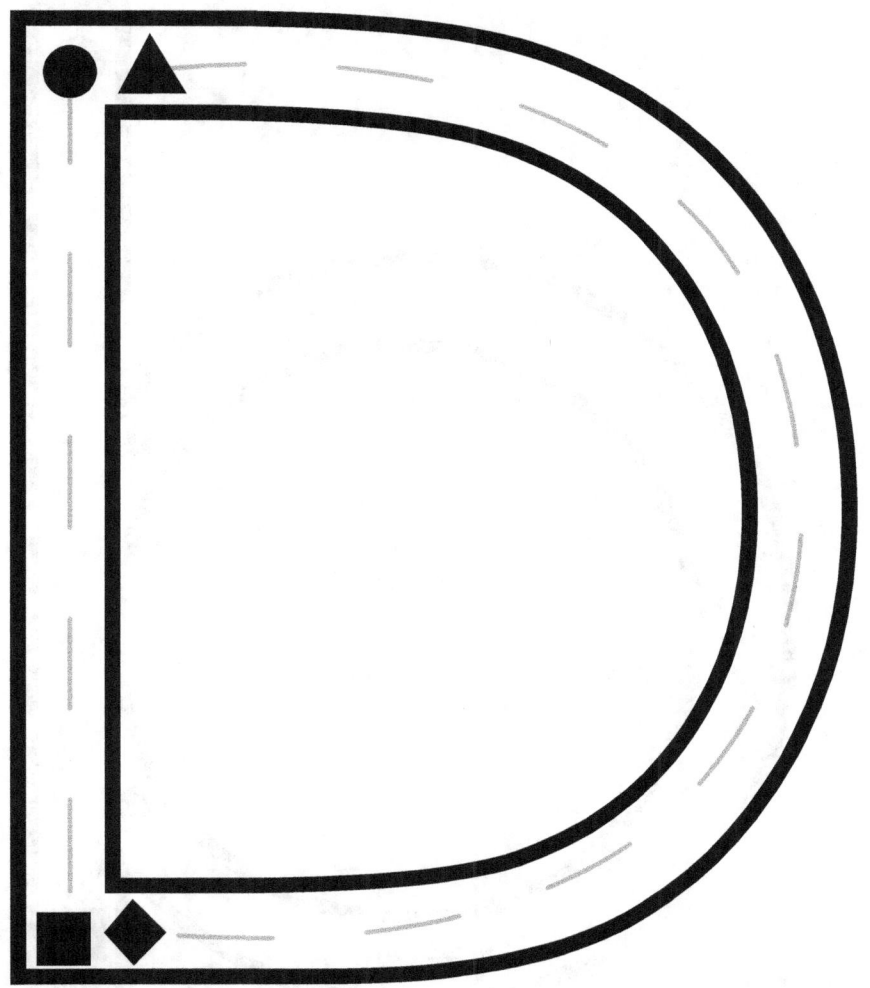

Practice tracing the uppercase D.

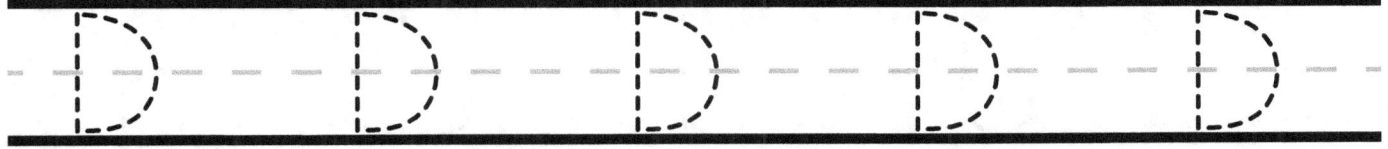

Now, try writing an uppercase D on your own.

Start at the ●. Trace the dotted line down to the ■. Place your pencil on the ▲, and follow the dotted line around to the ♦.

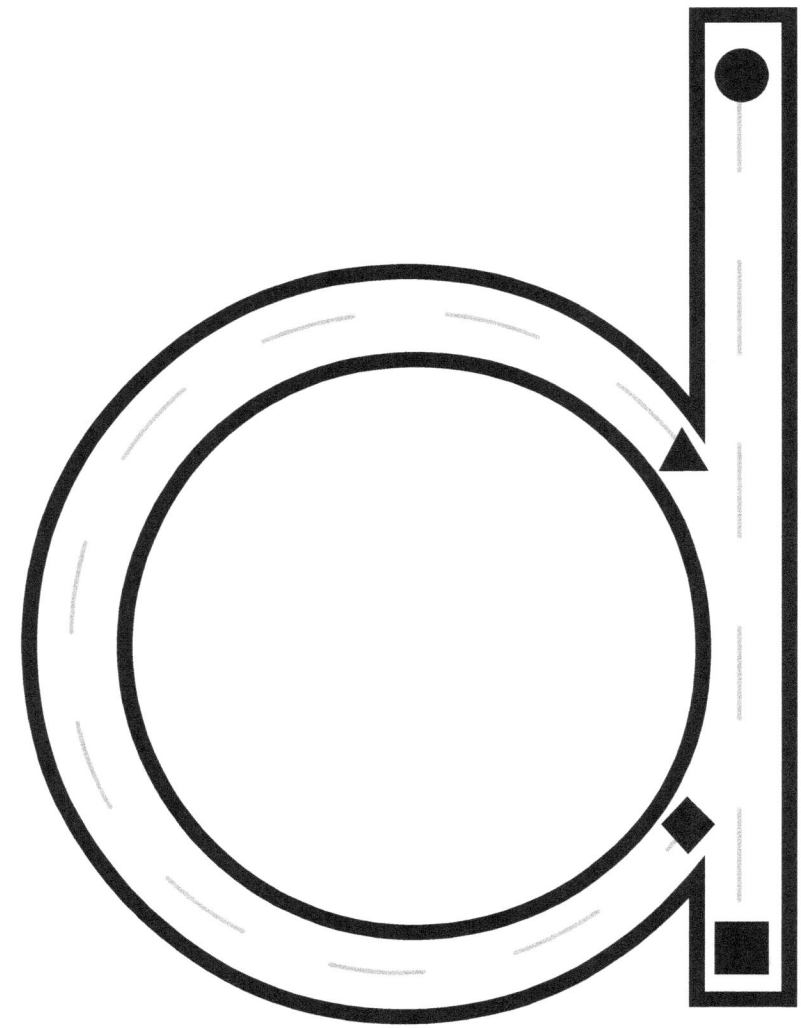

Practice tracing the lowercase d.

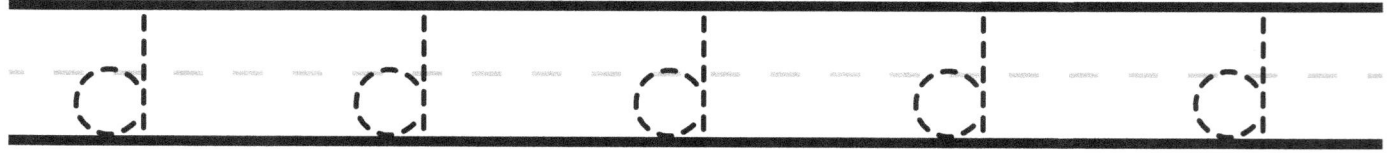

Now, try writing a lowercase d on your own.

Color the picture.

Color the uppercase E's blue. Color the lowercase e's yellow.

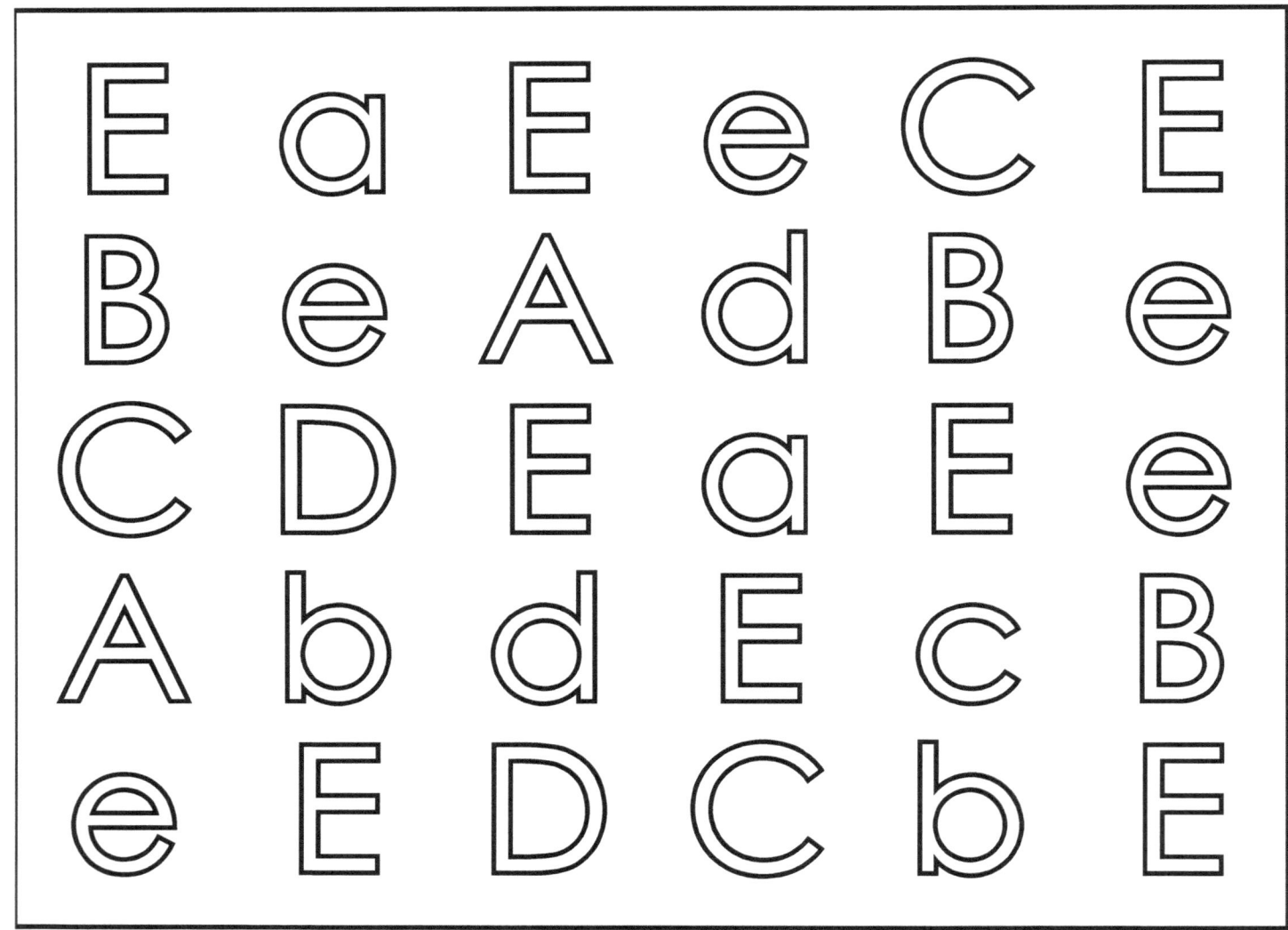

Start at the ●, trace over to the ■, down to the ▲, and over to the ♦. Place your pencil on the ♥, and trace across the the ★.

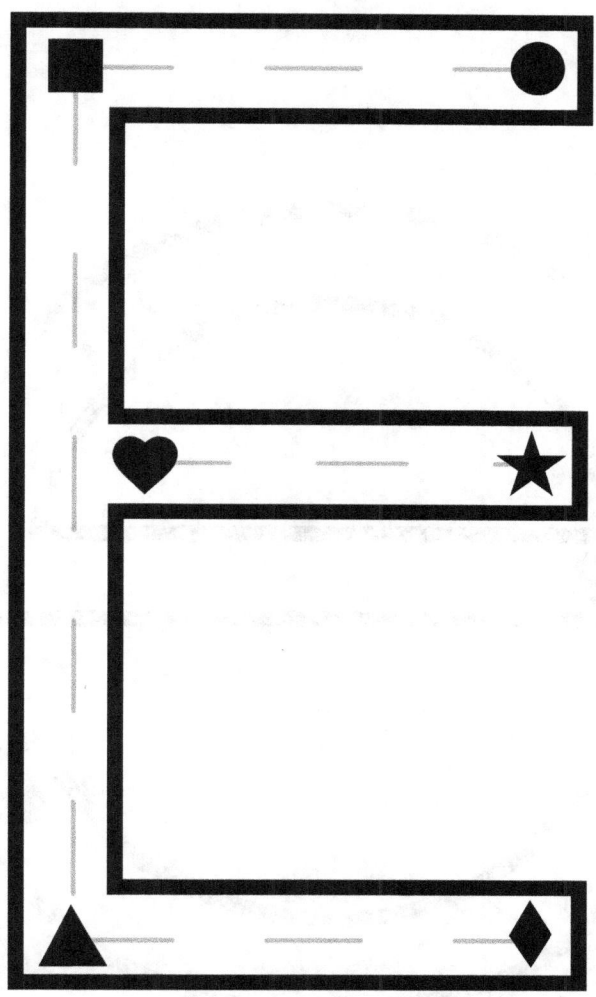

Practice tracing the uppercase E.

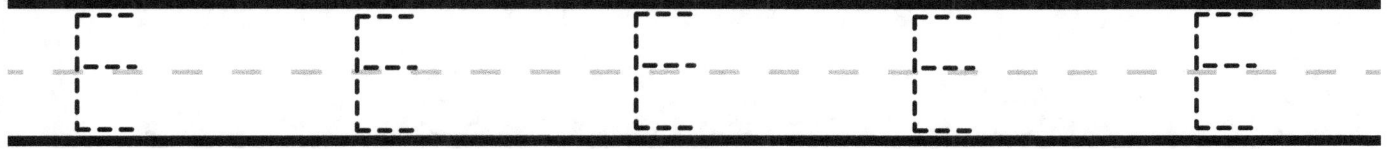

Now, try writing an uppercase E on your own.

Place your pencil on the ●. Trace the dotted line to the ■, and around to the ▲.

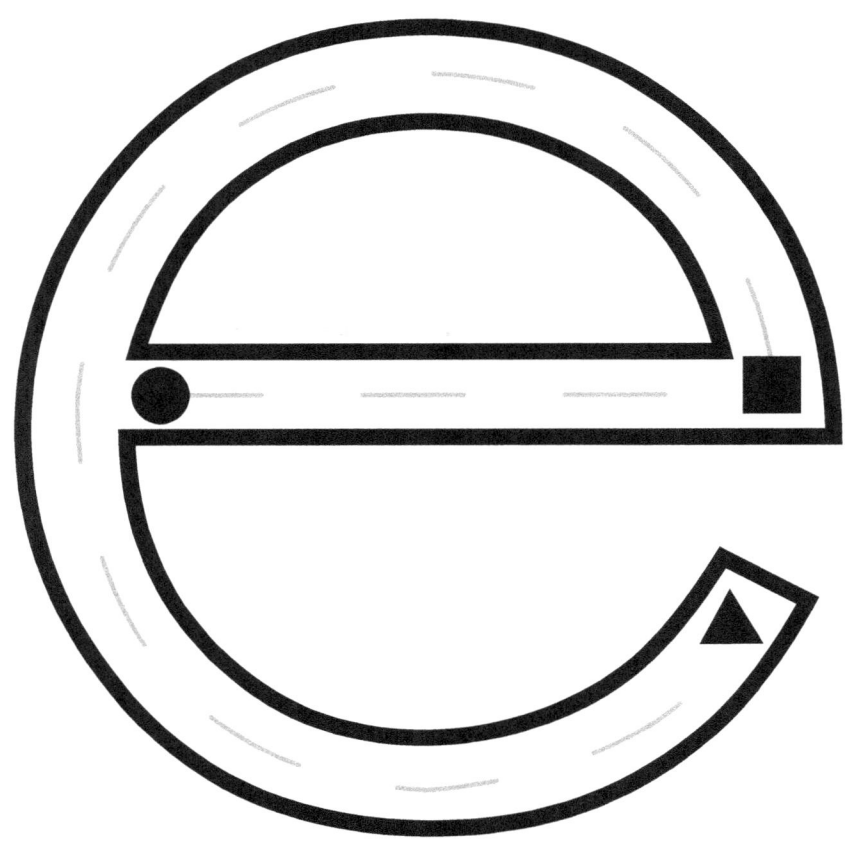

Practice tracing the lowercase e.

Now, try writing a lowercase e on your own.

Color the picture.

Circle the pictures that start with Ff.

Place your pencil on the ●. Trace the dotted line over to the ■ and down to the ▲. Place your pencil on the ♦. Trace over to the ♥.

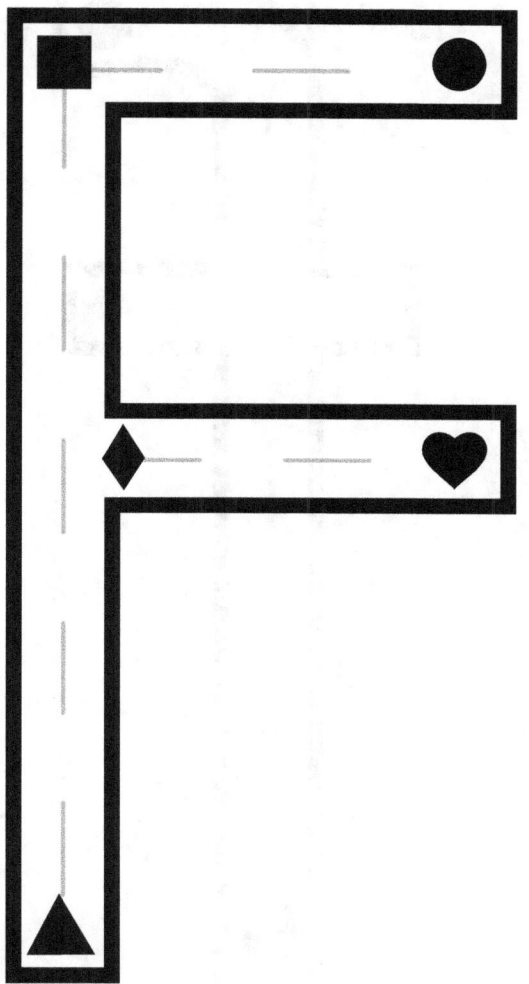

Practice tracing the uppercase F.

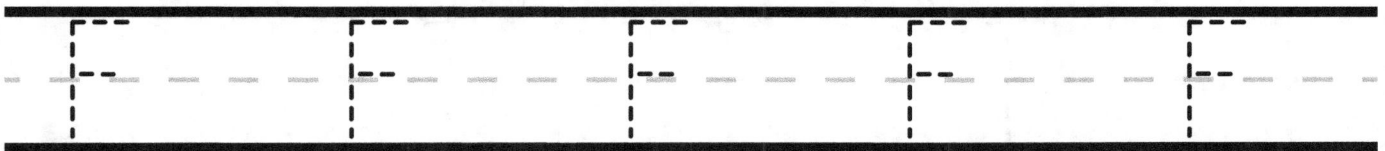

Now, try writing an uppercase F on your own.

Start on the ●. Trace around and down to the ■. Place your pencil on the ▲, and trace the dotted line to the ◆.

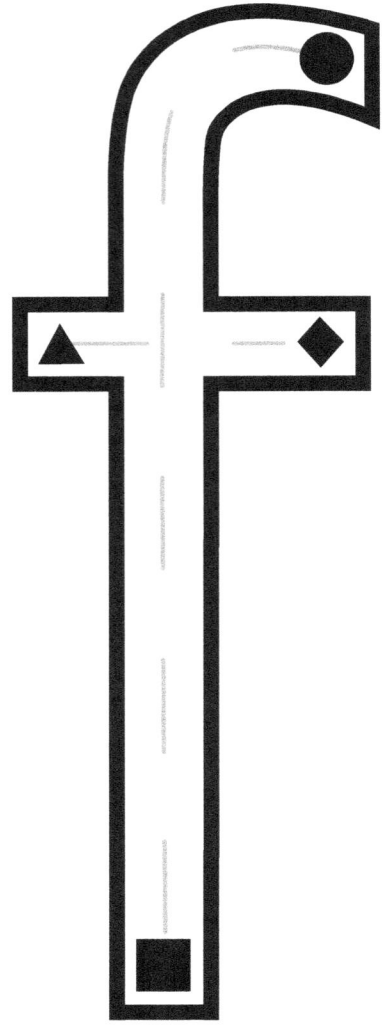

Practice tracing the lowercase f.

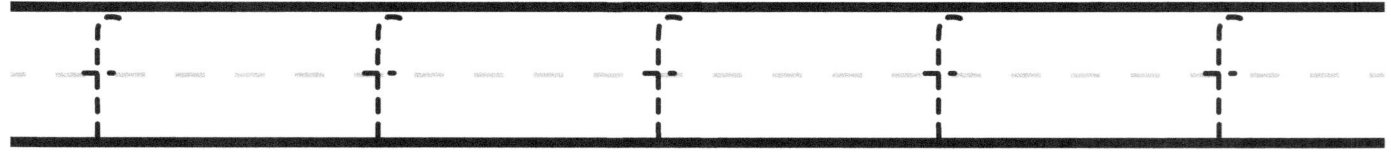

Now, try writing a lowercase f on your own.

Color the picture.

Help the **ghost** find his way to the **gift.**

Start at the ●, trace around to the ■, and over to the ▲.

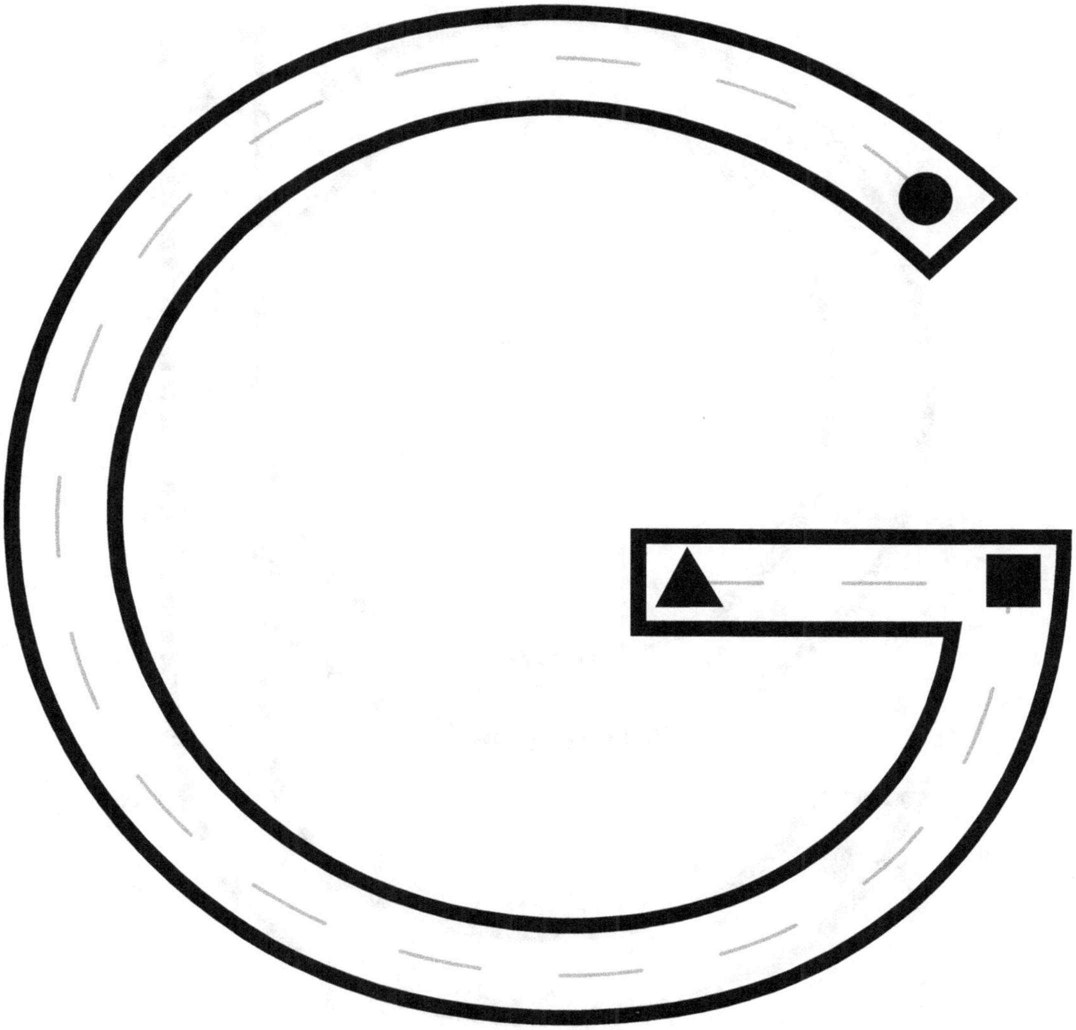

Practice tracing the uppercase G.

Now, try writing an uppercase G on your own.

Start at the ●, and trace the dotted line around to the ■. Place your pencil on the ▲. Follow the dotted line to the ◆.

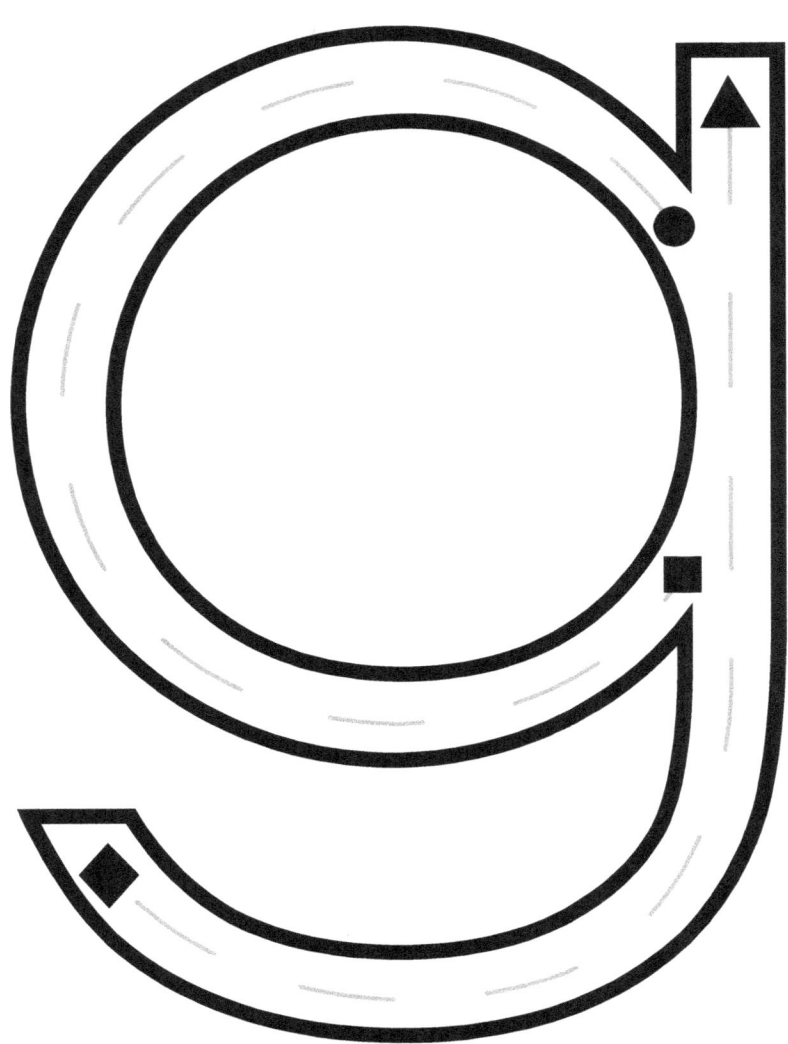

Practice tracing the lowercase g.

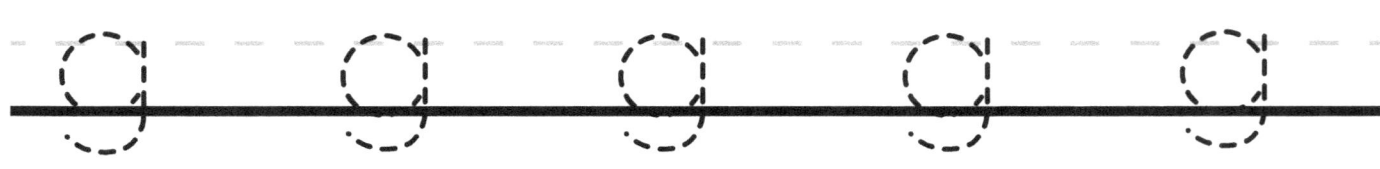

Now, try writing a lowercase g on your own.

Color the picture.

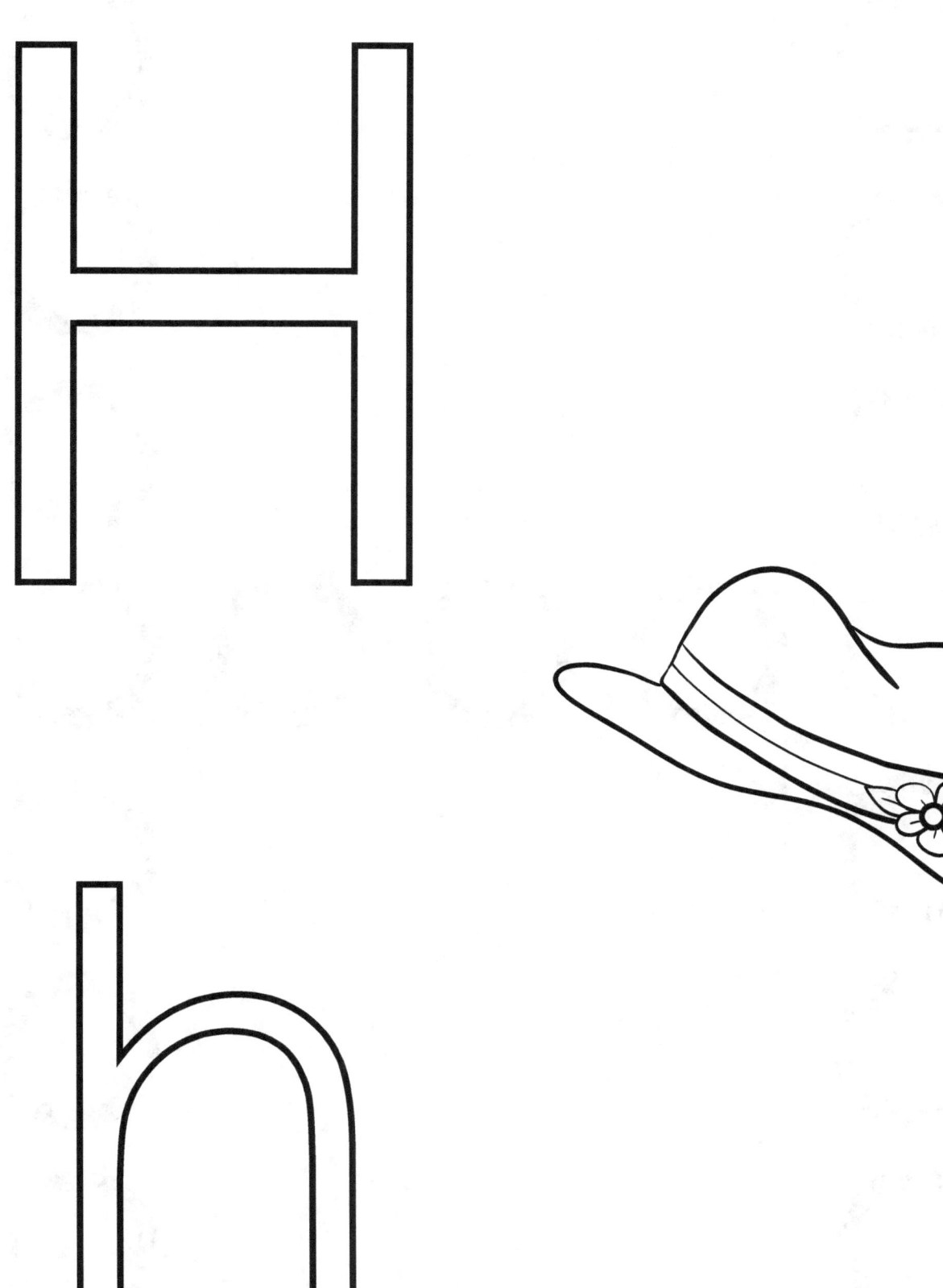

Dip a Q-tip in paint to dot each circle on the letter H.

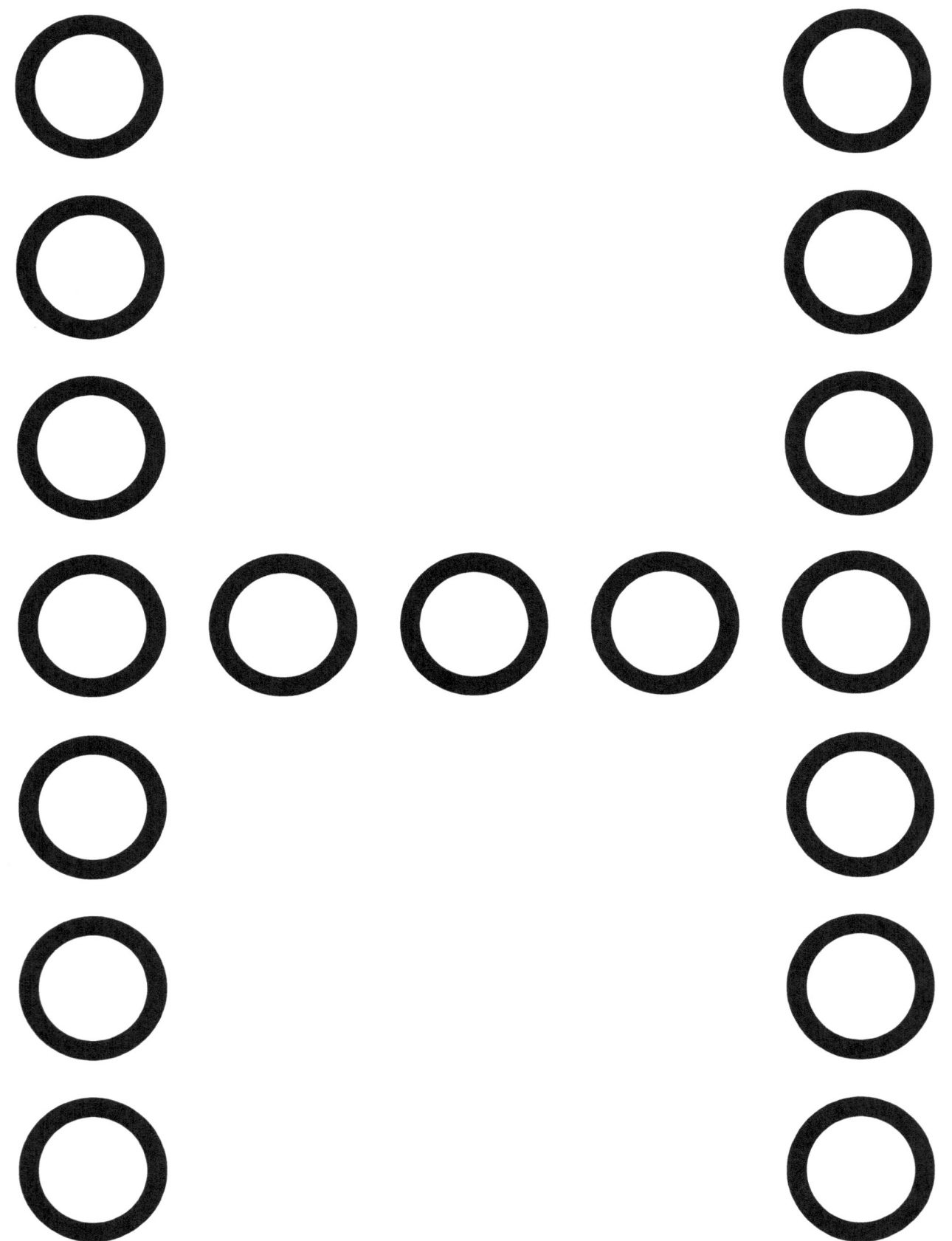

Start at the ●. Trace down to the ■. Place your pencil on the ▲, and trace down to the ♦. Place your pencil on the ♥, and trace across to the ★.

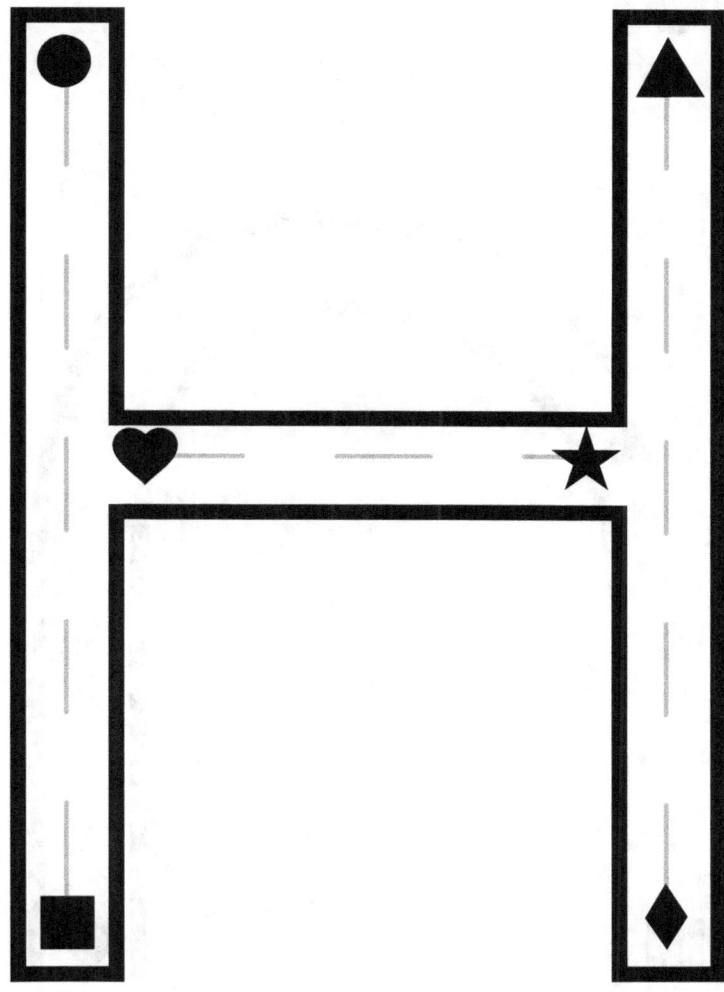

Practice tracing the uppercase H.

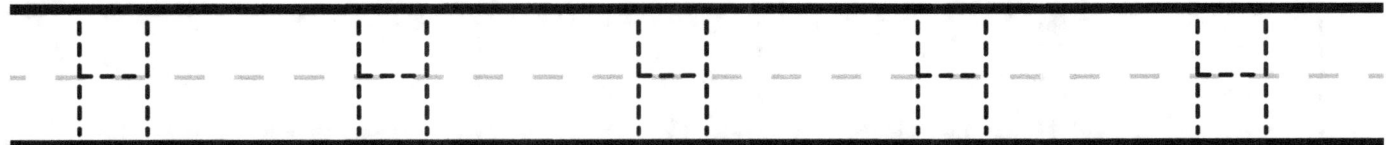

Now, try writing an uppercase H on your own.

Place your pencil on the ●. Follow the dotted line down to the ■.
Place your pencil on the ▲, and trace around to the ◆.

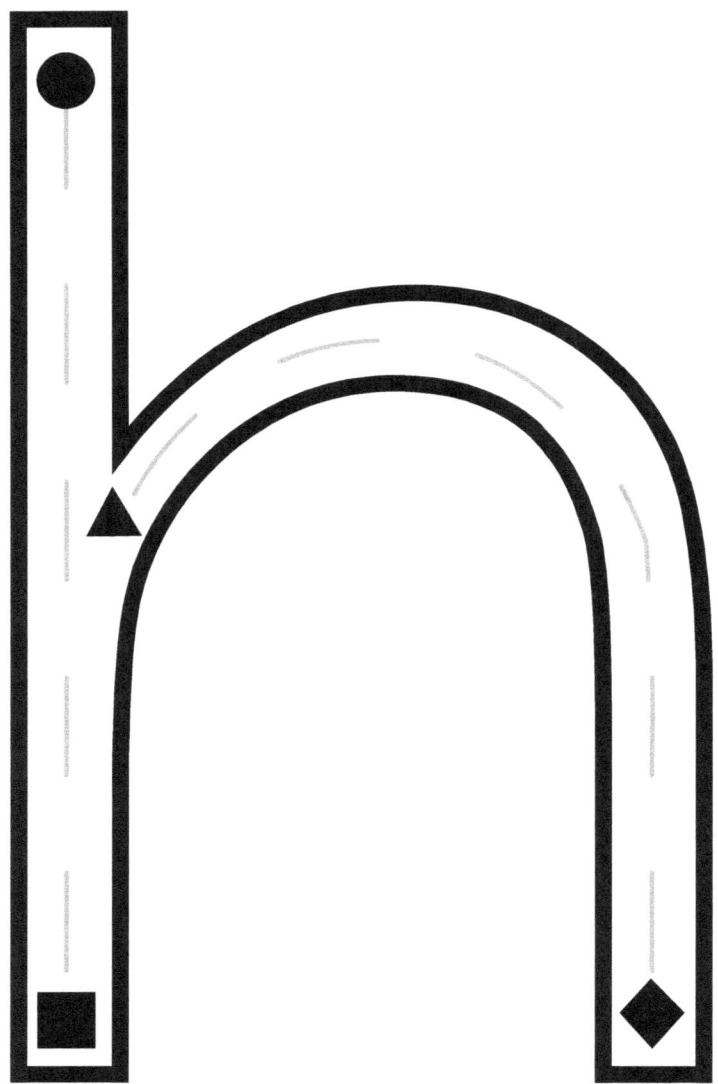

Practice tracing the lowercase h.

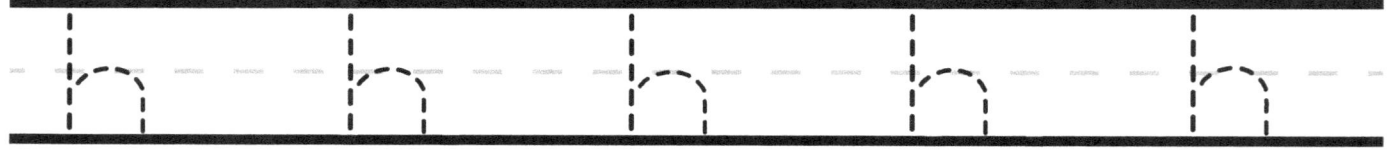

Now, try writing a lowercase h on your own.

Learning ABC's Workbook: Print | Autumn McKay

Color the picture.

Left blank for cutting purposes.

Cut out the letter I.

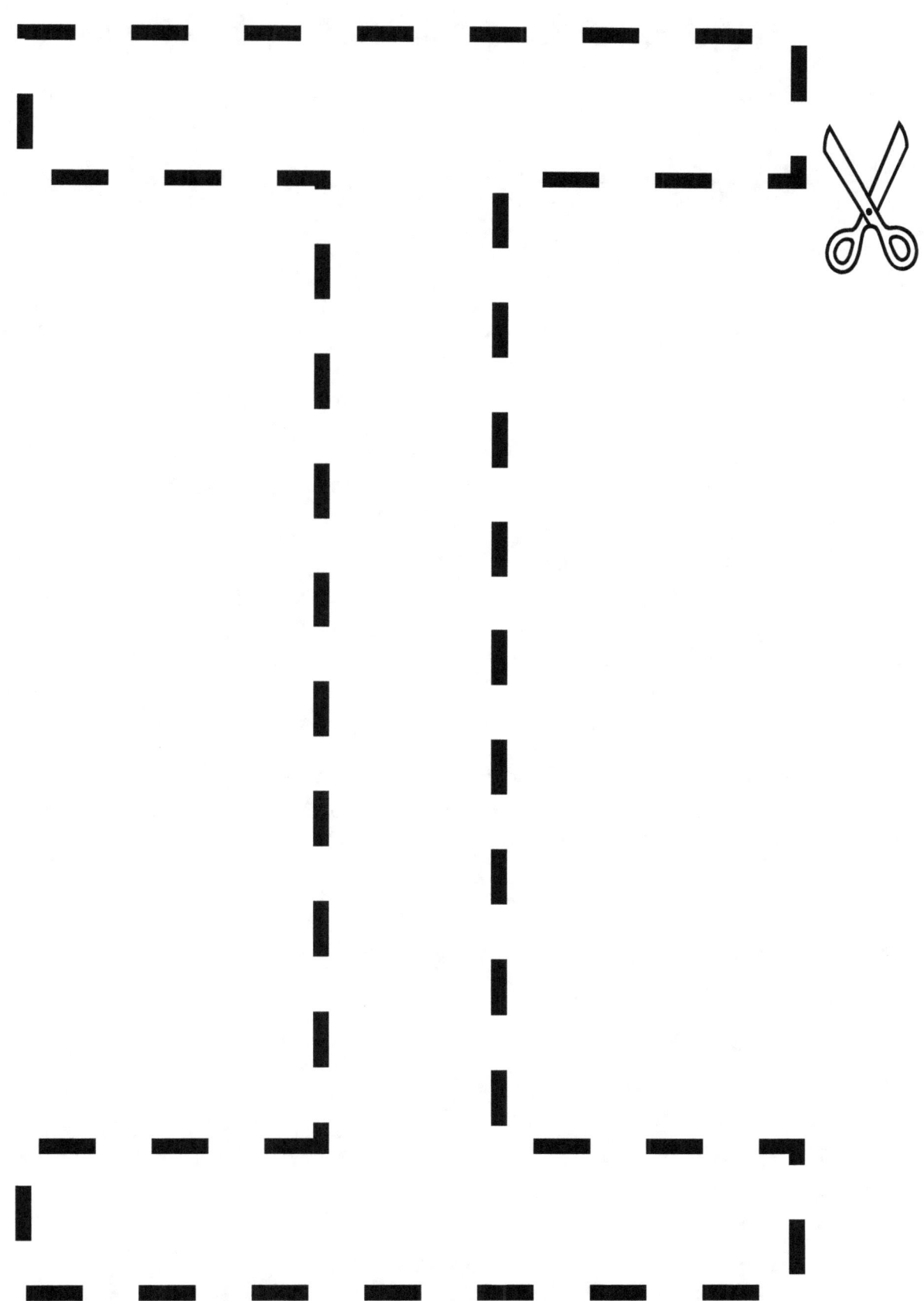

Left blank for cutting purposes.

Place your pencil on the ●, and trace down to the ■. Place your pencil on the ▲, and trace across to the ♦. Place your pencil on the ♥, and trace across to the ★.

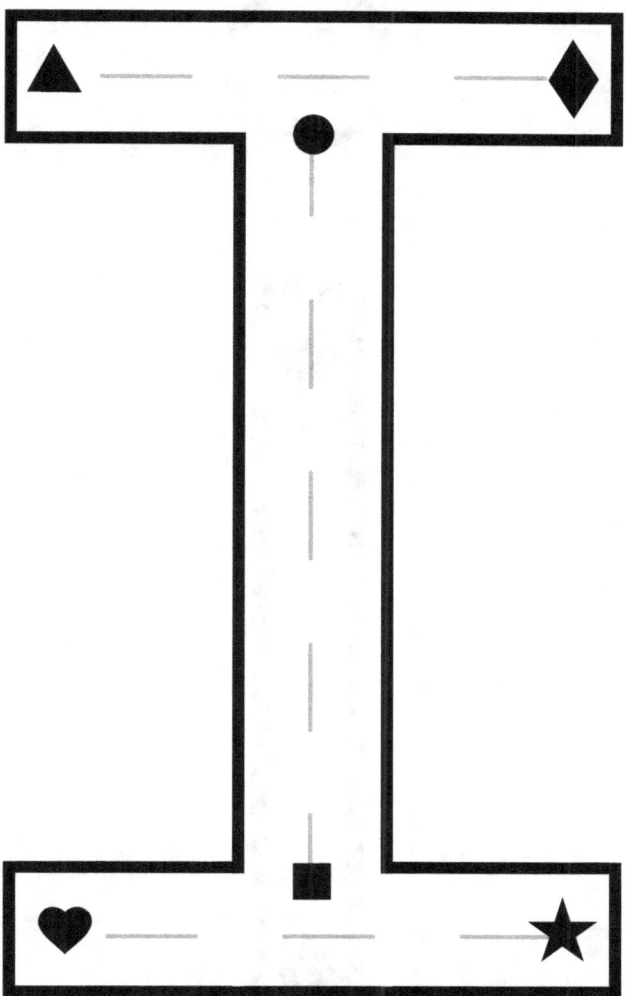

Practice tracing the uppercase I.

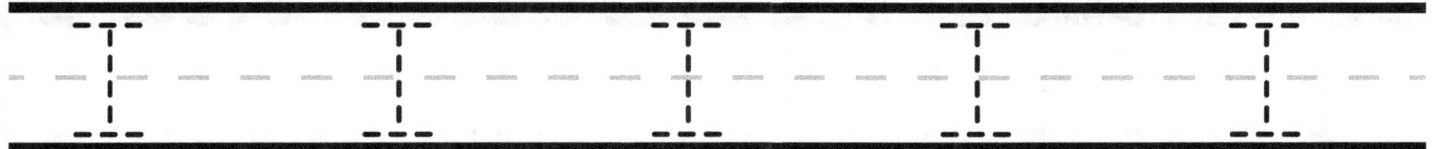

Now, try writing and uppercase I on your own.

Start at the ●, and trace down to the ■. Place your pencil on the ▲ to make a dot.

Practice tracing the lowercase i.

Now, try writing a lowercase i on your own.

Color the picture.

J

j

Find the hidden picture by coloring all of the uppercase J's and lowercase j's in the picture.

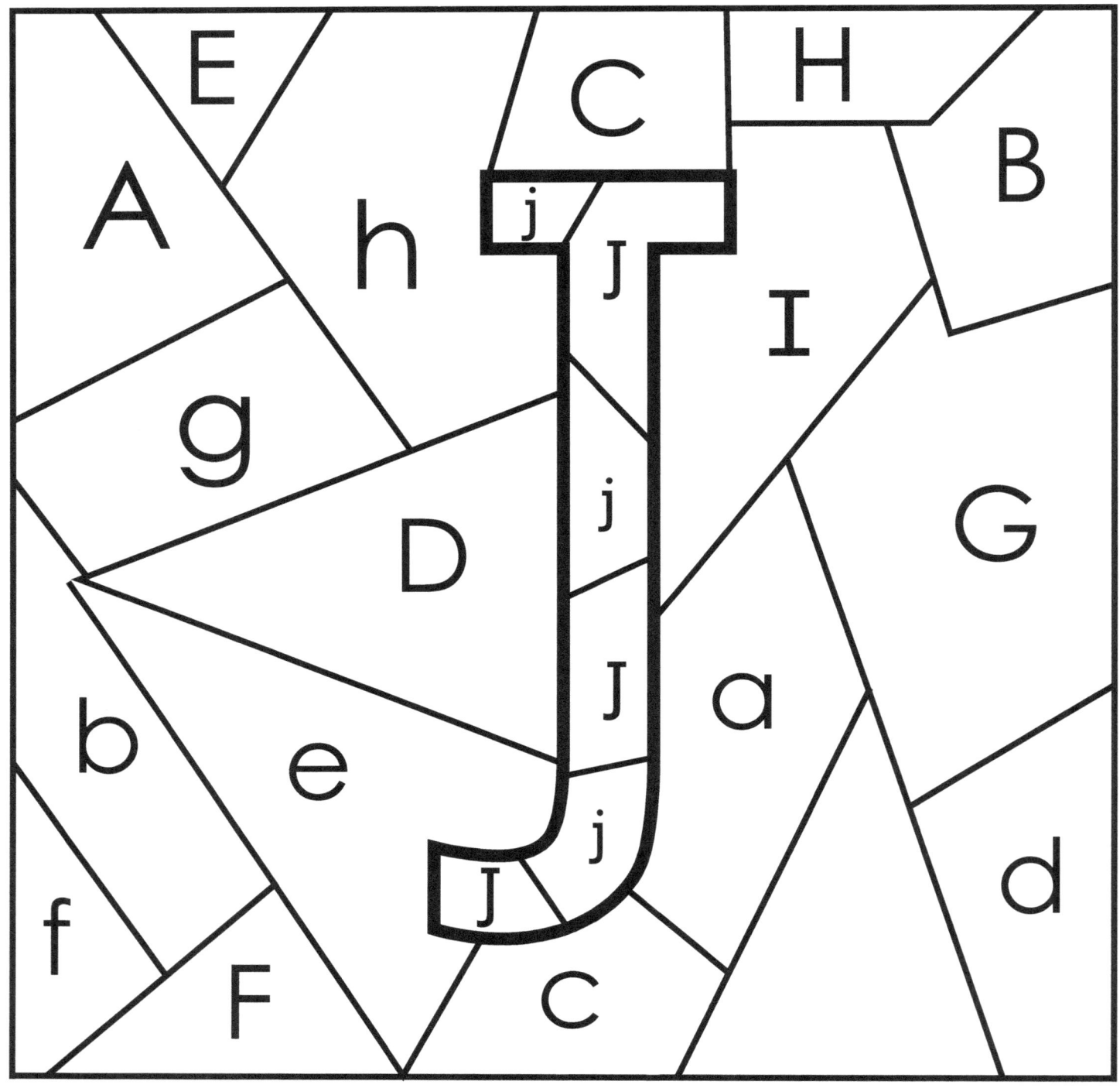

Start at the ●, and trace down and around to the ■. Place your pencil on the ▲, and trace across to the ♦.

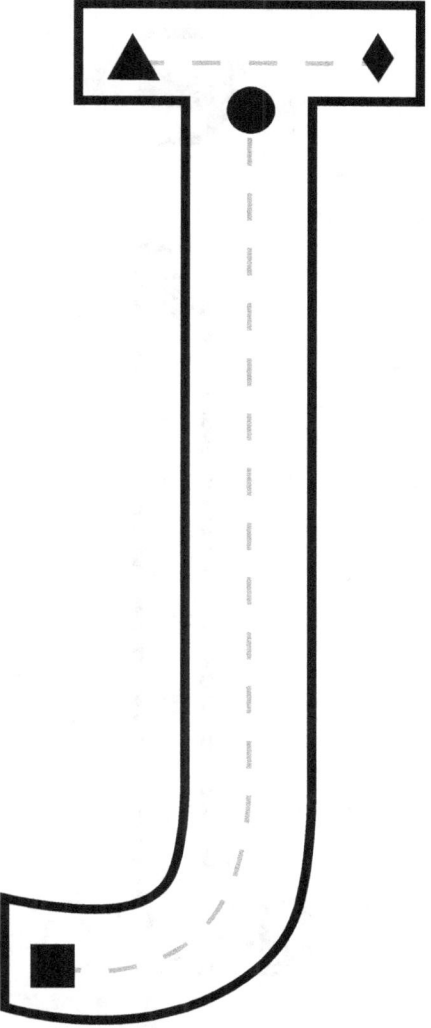

Practice tracing the uppercase J.

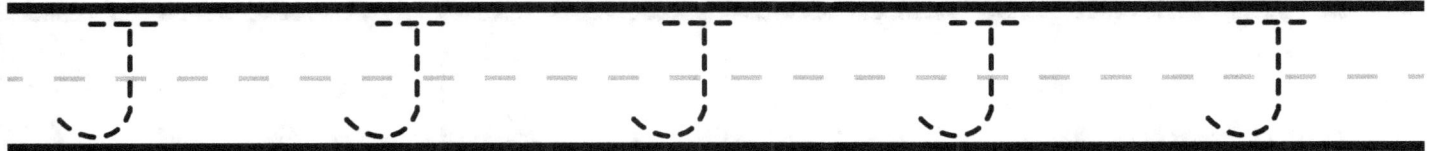

Now, try writing an uppercase J on your own.

Place your pencil on the ●. Trace the dotted line around to the ■.
Place your pencil on the ▲ to form a dot.

Practice tracing the lowercase j.

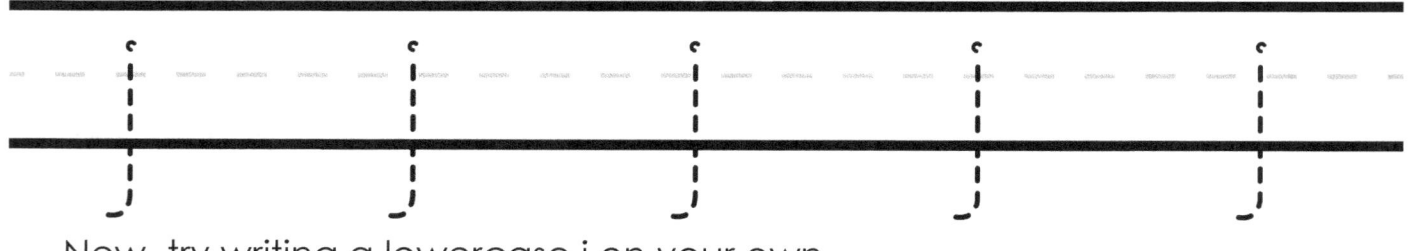

Now, try writing a lowercase j on your own.

Color the picture.

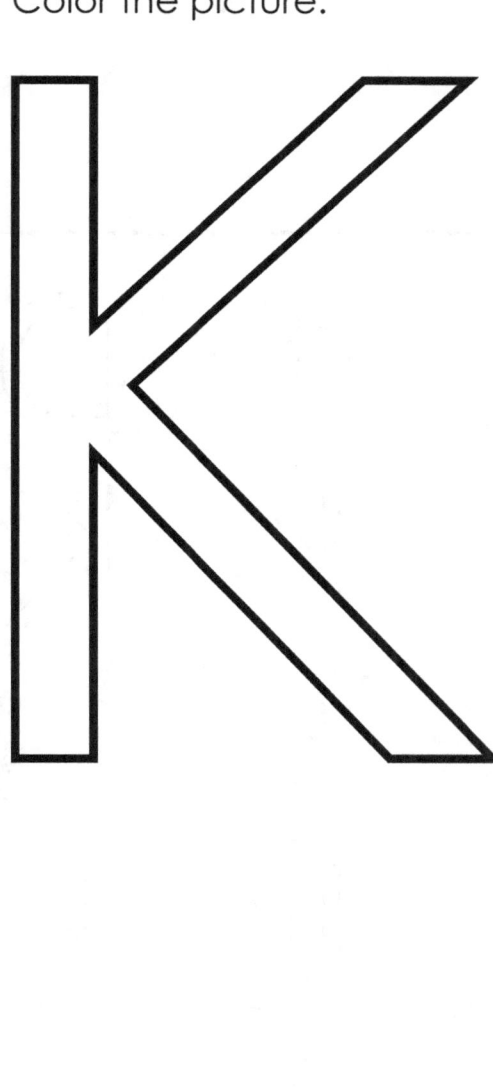

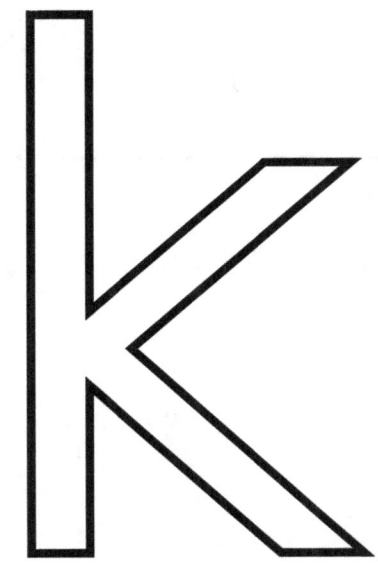

Color the uppercase K's green. Color the lowercase k's red.

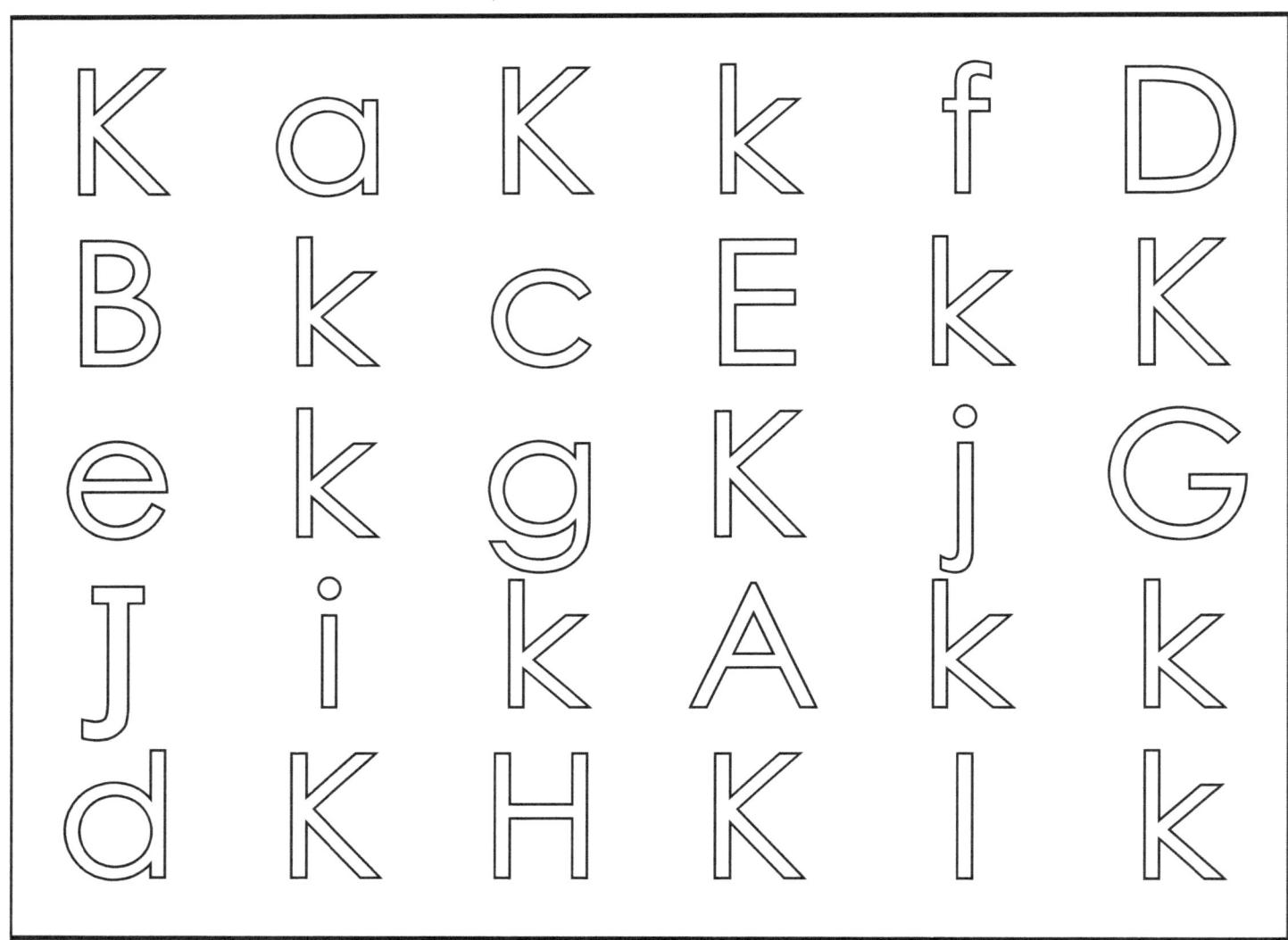

Place your pencil on the ●, and trace the dotted line down to the ■.
Place your pencil on the ▲. Trace down to the ♦ and down to the ♥.

Practice tracing the uppercase K.

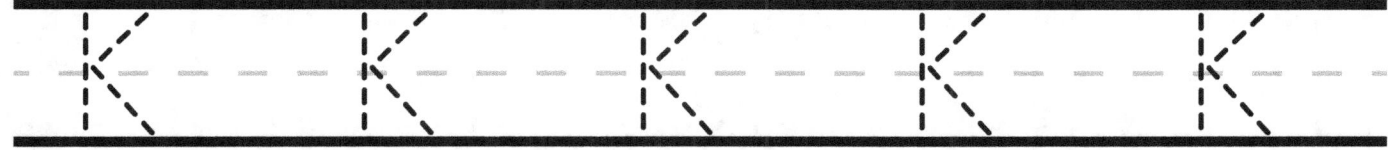

Now, try writing an uppercase K on your own.

Start at the ●. Trace down to the ■. Place your pencil on the ▲. Trace down to the ♦ and down to the ♥.

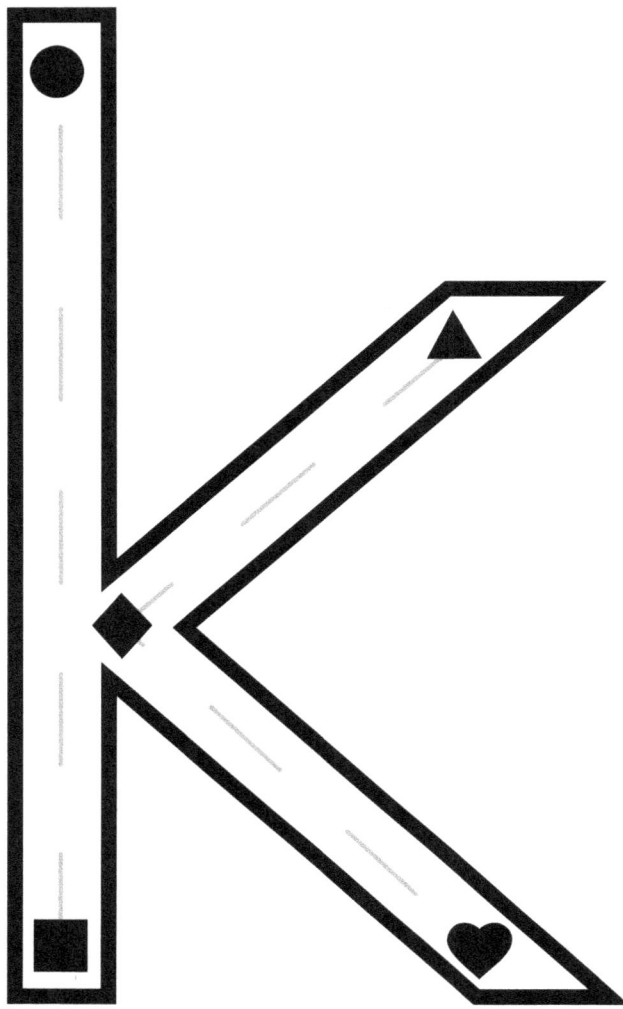

Practice tracing the lowercase k.

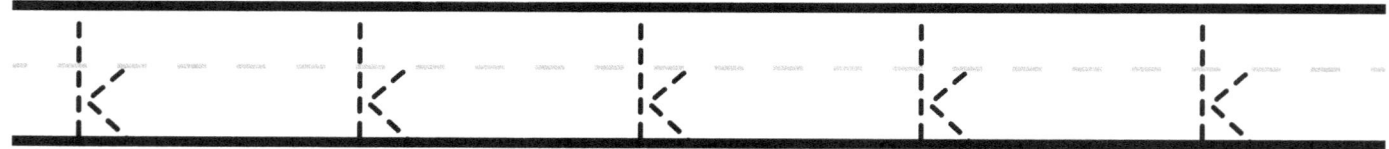

Now, try writing a lowercase k on your own.

Color the picture.

Circle the pictures that start with Ll.

Start at the ●. Trace down to the ■, and over to the ▲.

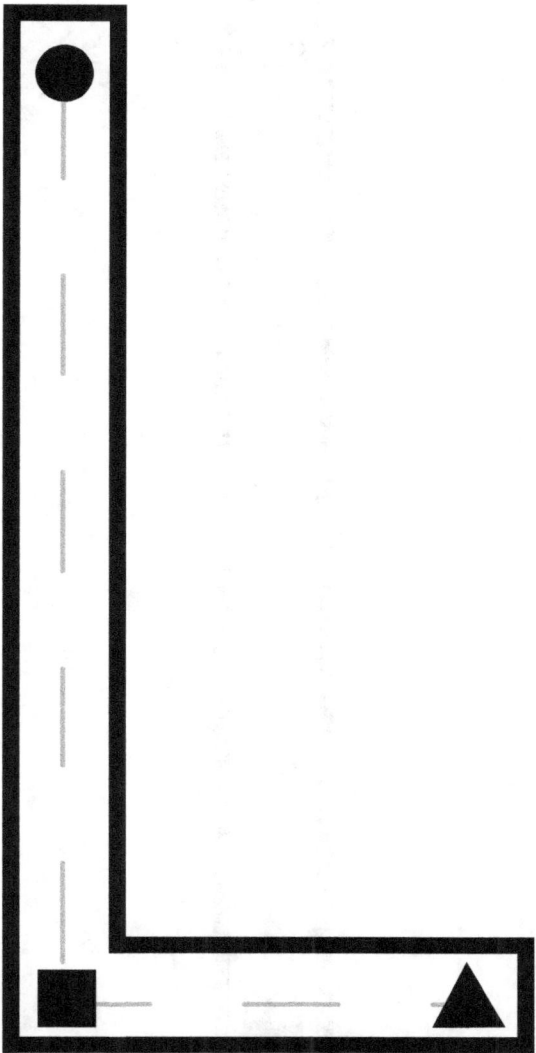

Practice tracing the uppercase L.

Now, try writing an uppercase L on your own.

Start at the ●, and trace down to the ■.

Practice tracing the lowercase l.

Now, try writing a lowercase l on your own.

Color the picture.

Help the **monkey** find his way through the maze to his **muffin**.

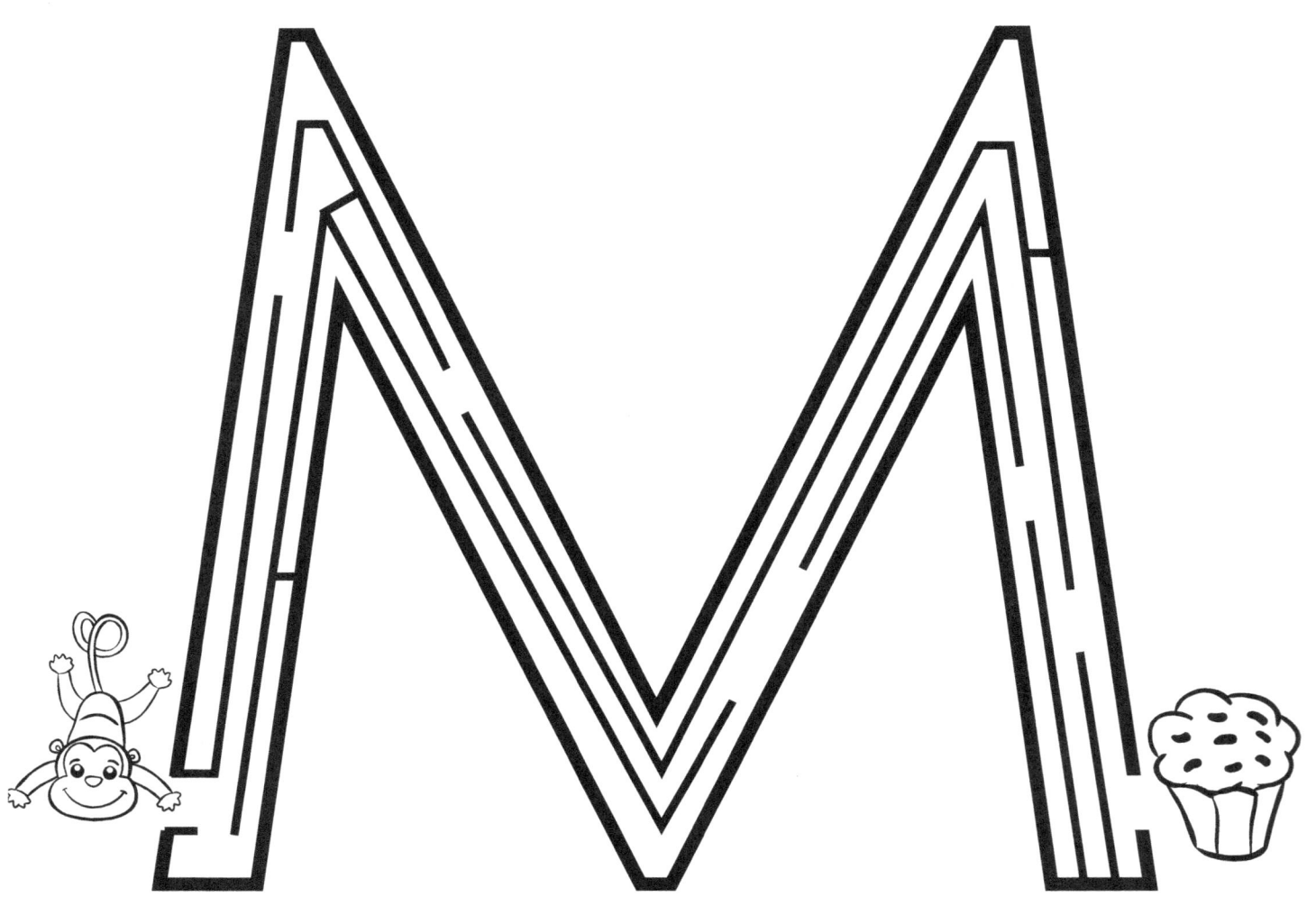

Start at the ●. Trace the dotted line up to the ■, down to the ▲, up to the ◆, and down to the ♥.

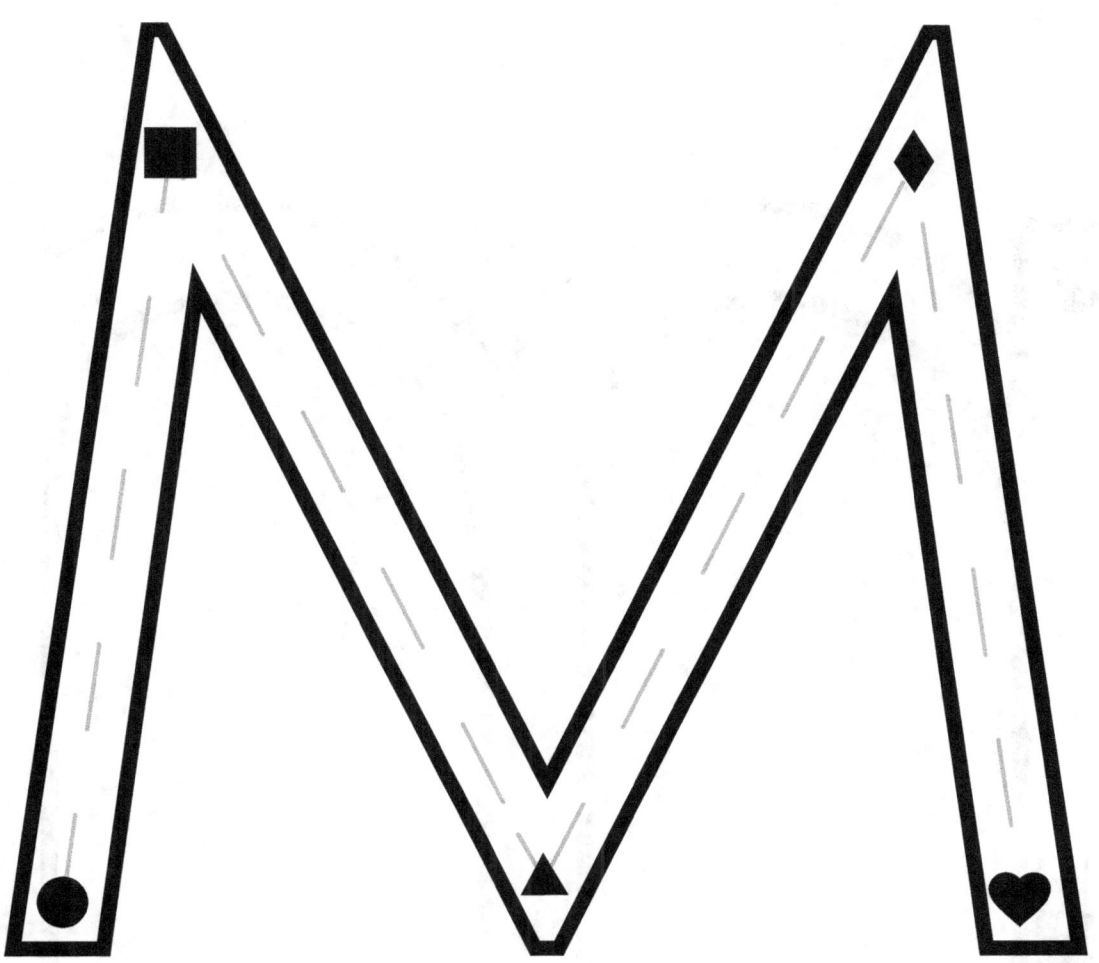

Practice tracing the uppercase M.

Now, try writing an uppercase M on your own.

Start at the ●. Trace down to the ■. Place your pencil on the ▲. Trace around to the ♦ and around to the ♥.

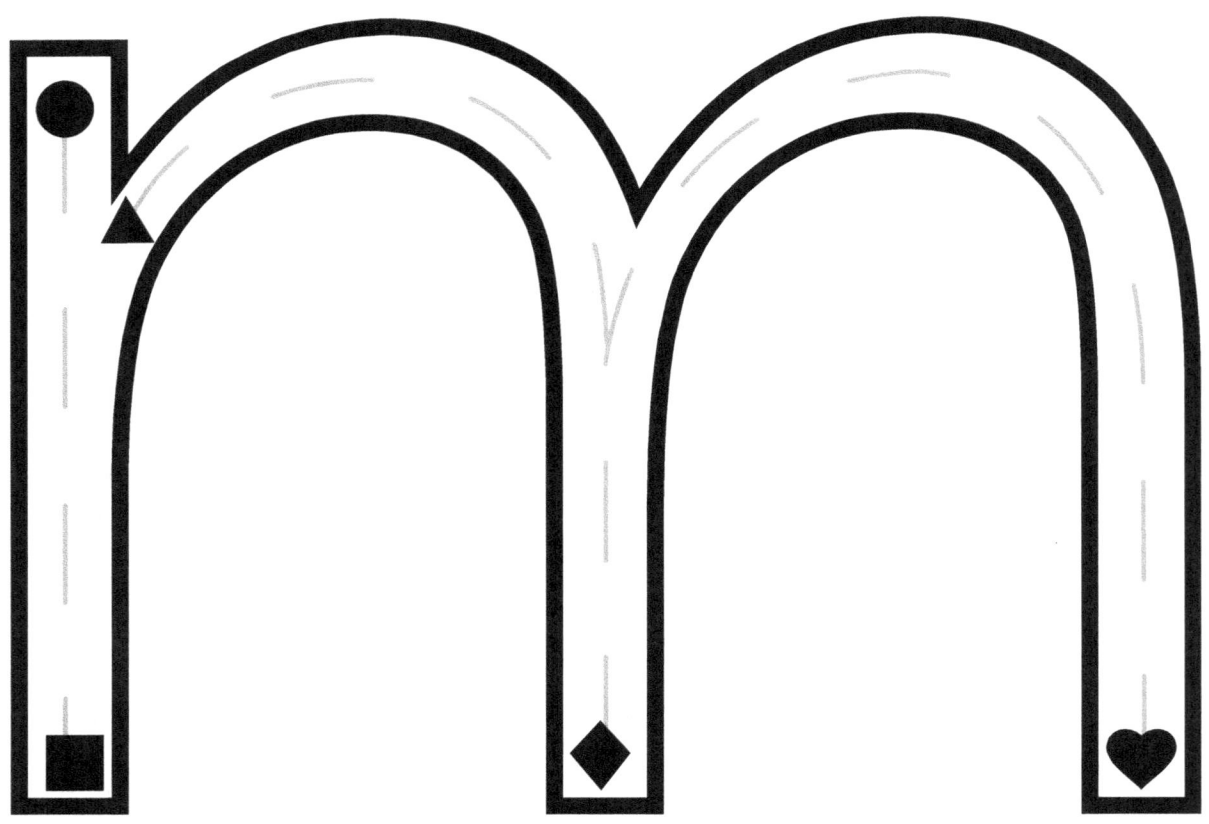

Practice tracing the lowercase m.

Now, try writing a lowercase m on your own.

Color the picture.

Color the uppercase N's red. Color the lowercase n's purple.

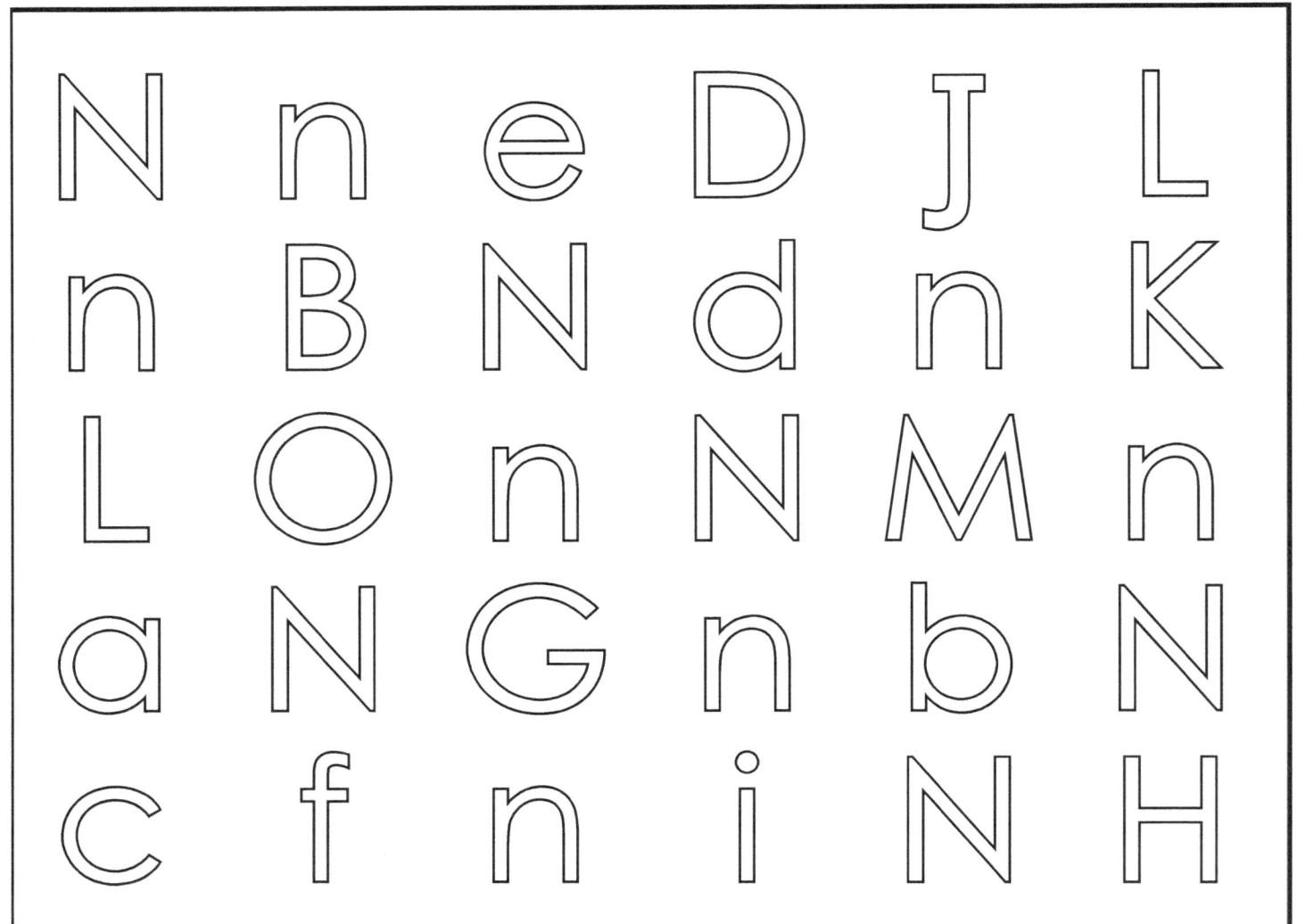

Place your pencil on the ●. Trace the line up to the ■, down to the ▲, and up to the ♦.

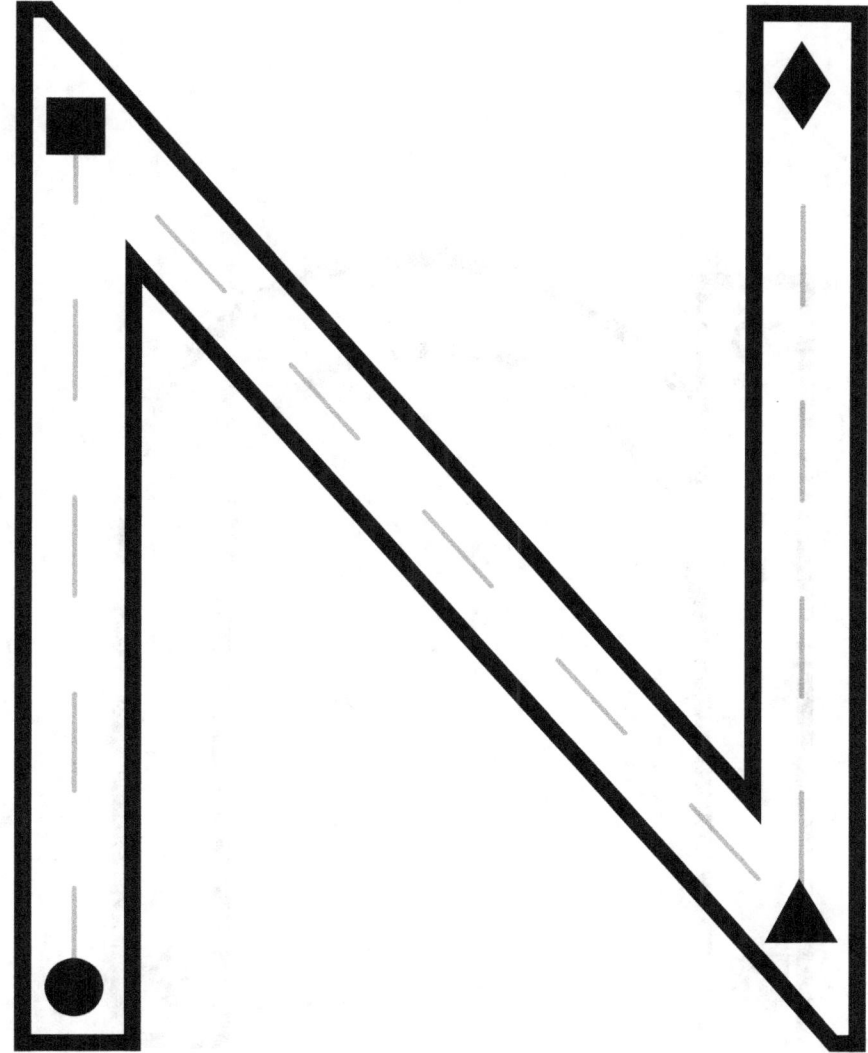

Practice tracing the uppercase N.

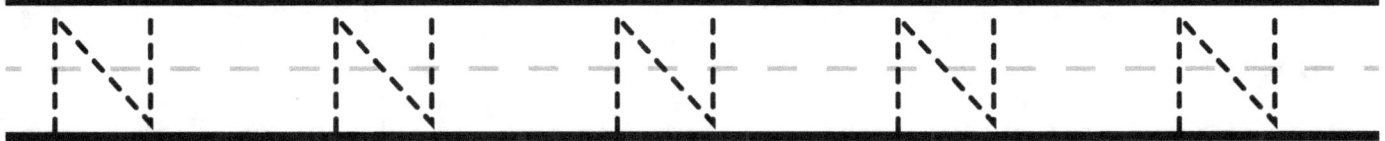

Now, try writing an uppercase N on your own.

Start at the ●. Trace down to the ■. Place your pencil on the ▲, and trace around to the ♦.

Practice tracing the lowercase n.

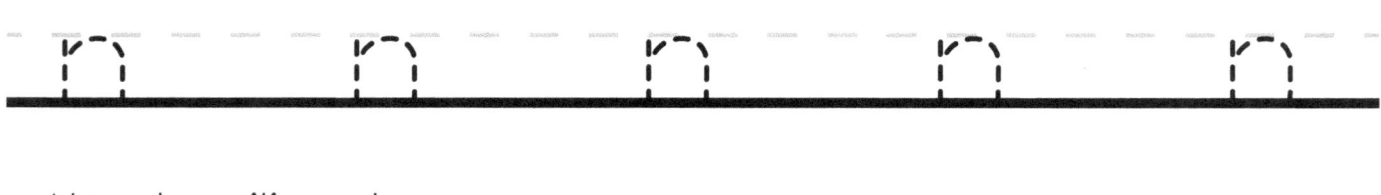

Now, try writing a lowercase n on your own.

Color the picture.

Dip your finger in paint to dot each circle on the letter O.

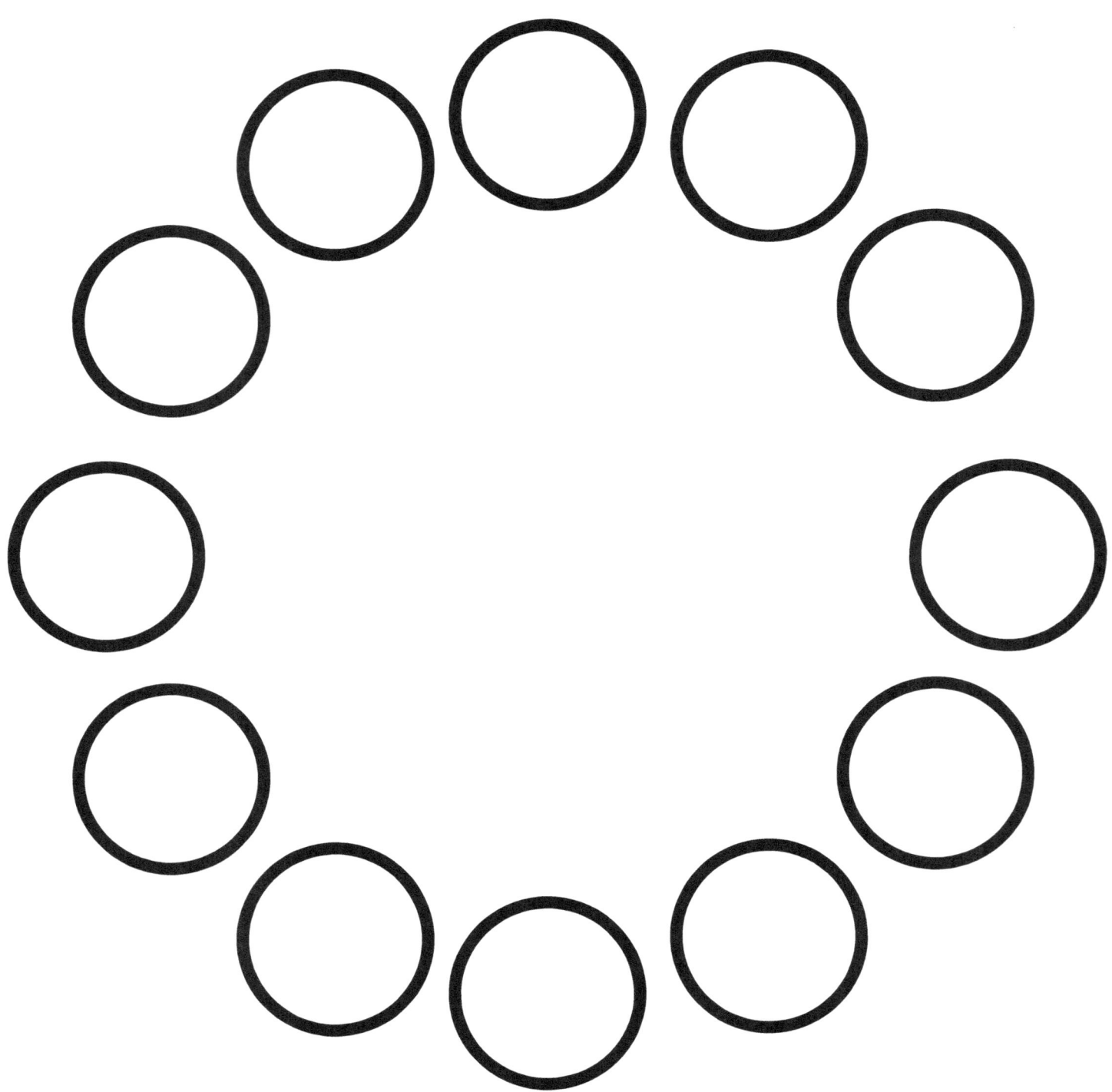

Start at the ●. Trace the dotted line around to the ■.

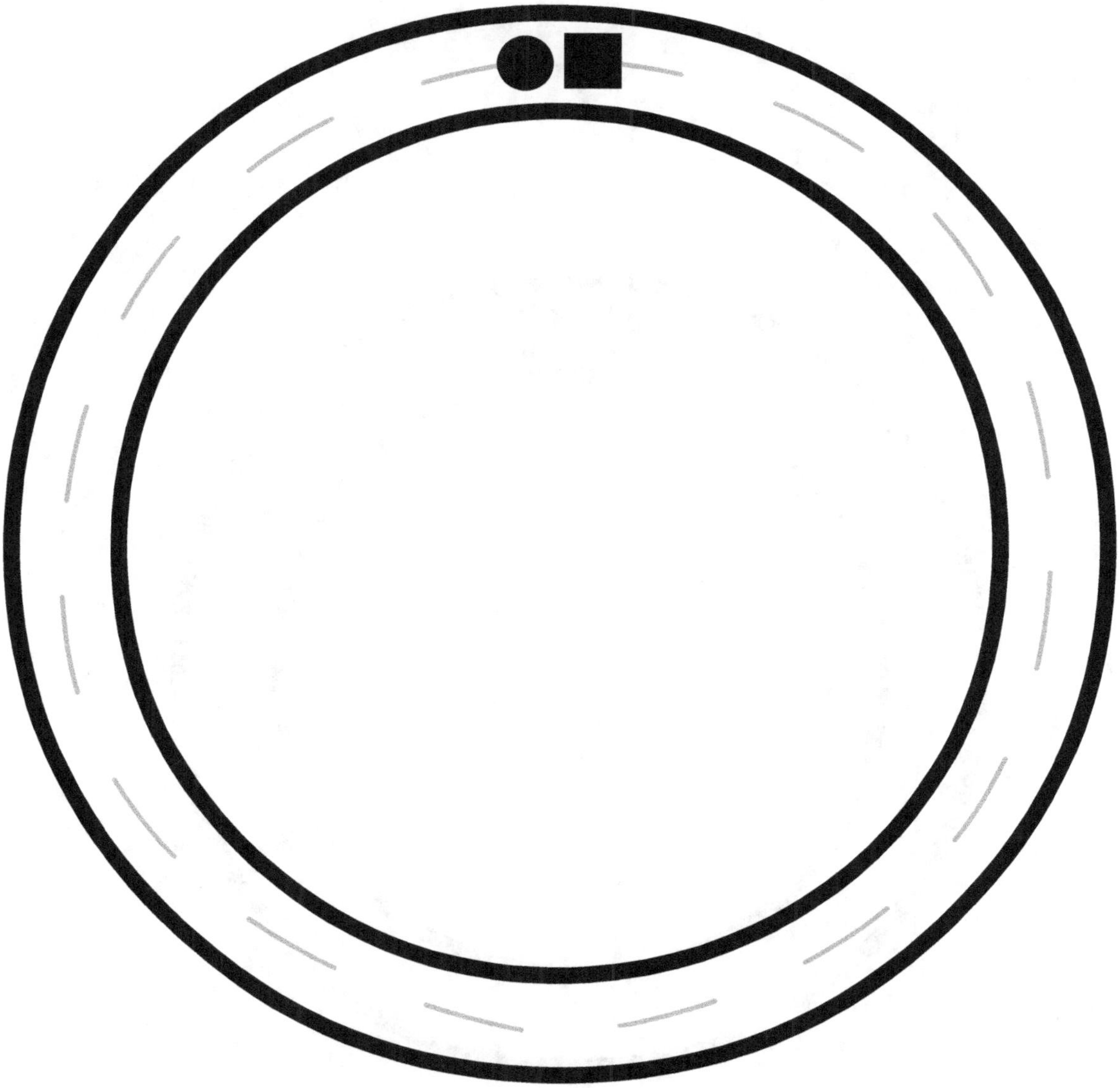

Practice tracing the uppercase O.

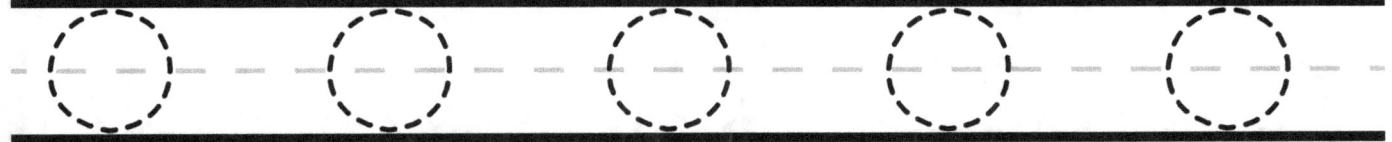

Now, try writing an uppercase O on your own.

Start at the ●. Trace the dotted line around to the ■.

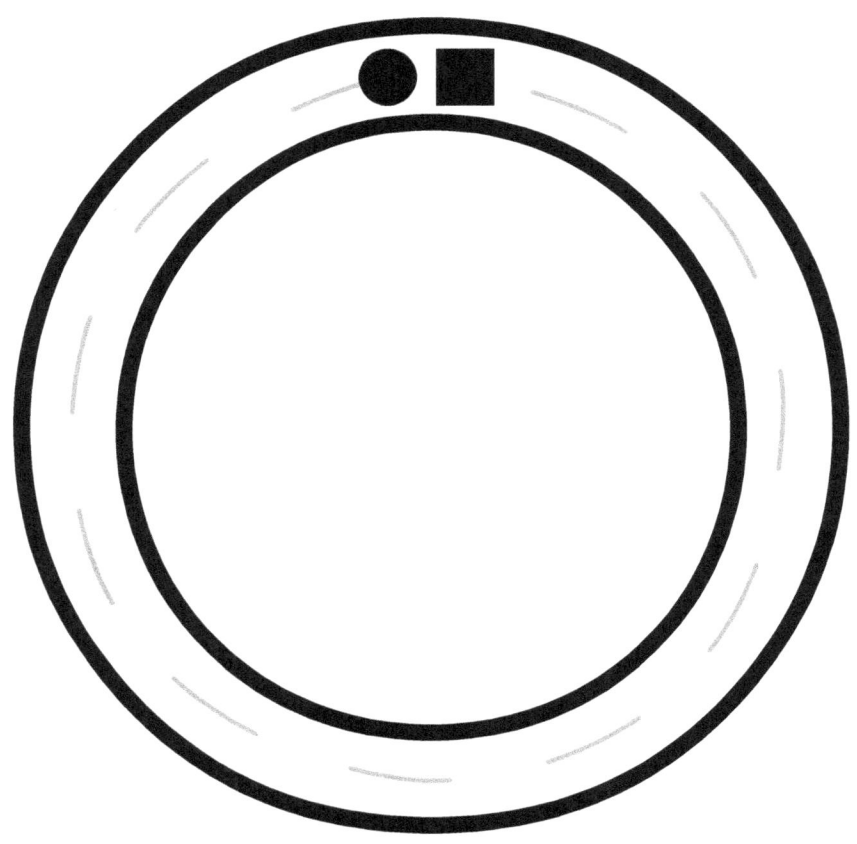

Practice tracing the lowercase o.

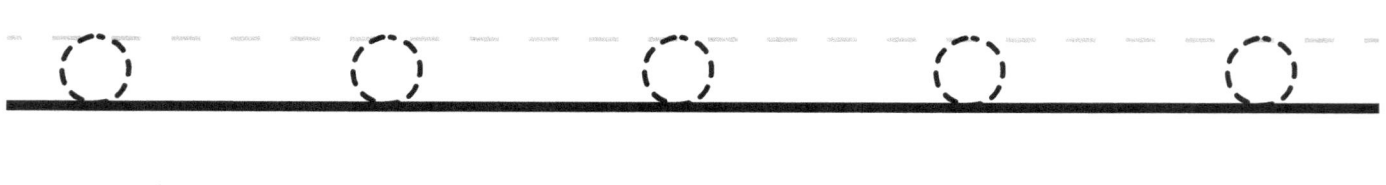

Now, try writing a lowercase o on your own.

Color the picture.

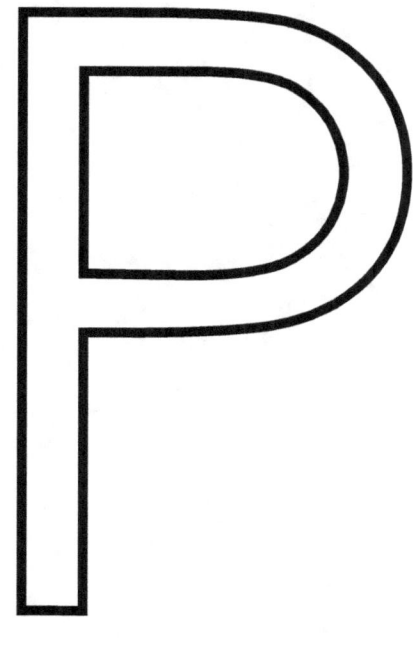

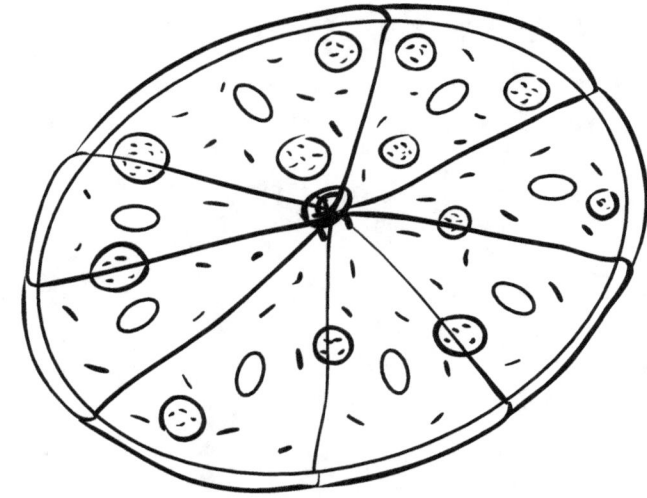

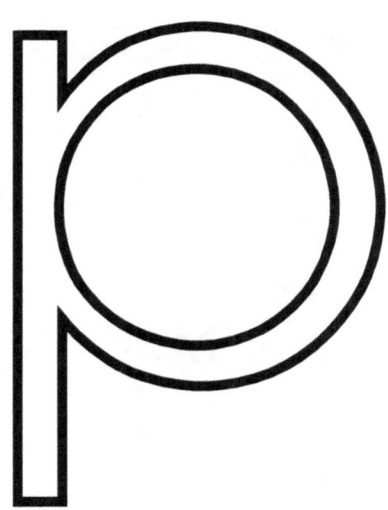

Left blank for cutting purposes.

Cut out the letter P.

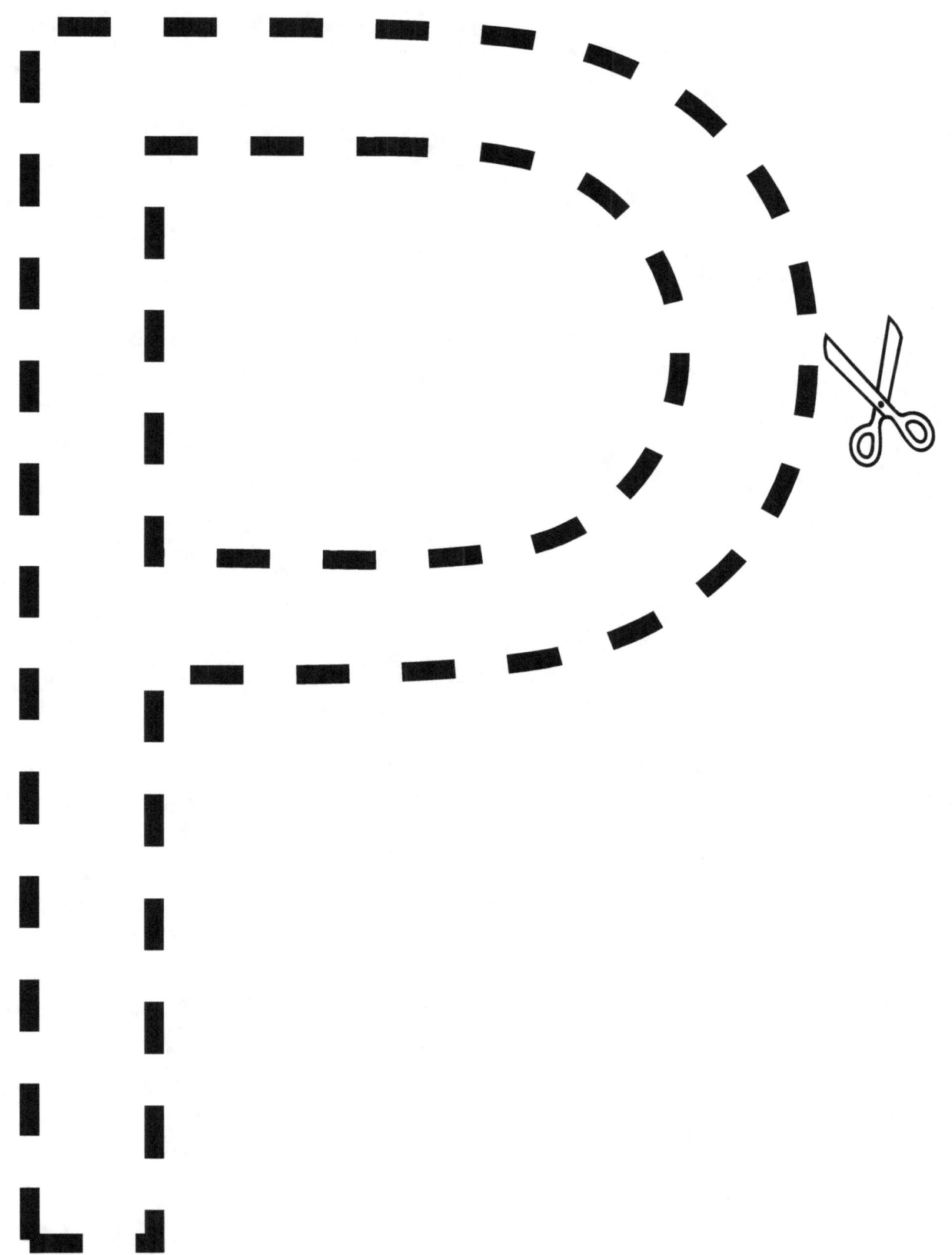

Left blank for cutting purposes.

Place your pencil on the ●, and trace down to the ■. Place your pencil on the ▲, and trace aroung to the ◆.

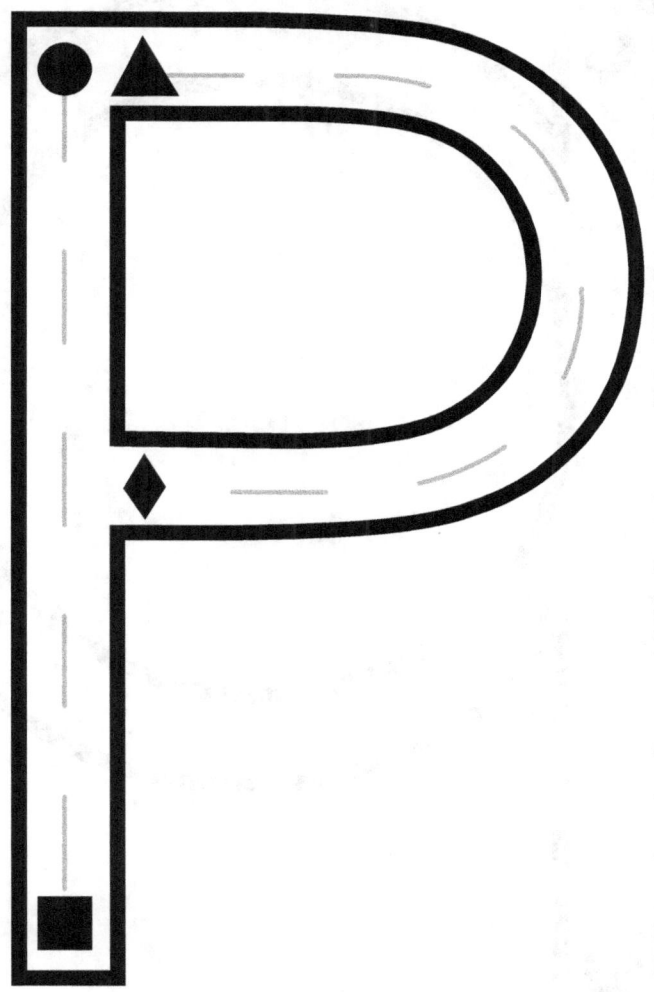

Practice tracing the uppercase P.

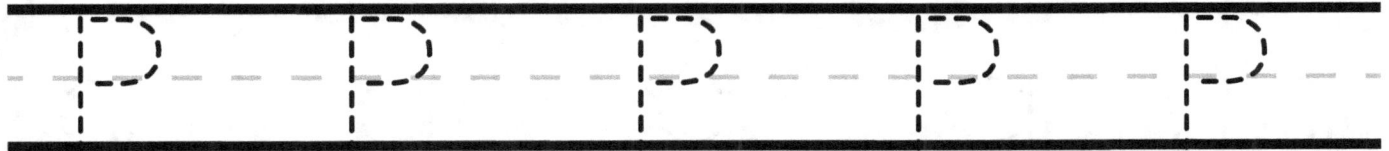

Now, trying writing an uppercase P on your own.

Place your pencil on the ●, and trace down to the ■. Place your pencil on the ▲, and trace aroung to the ♦.

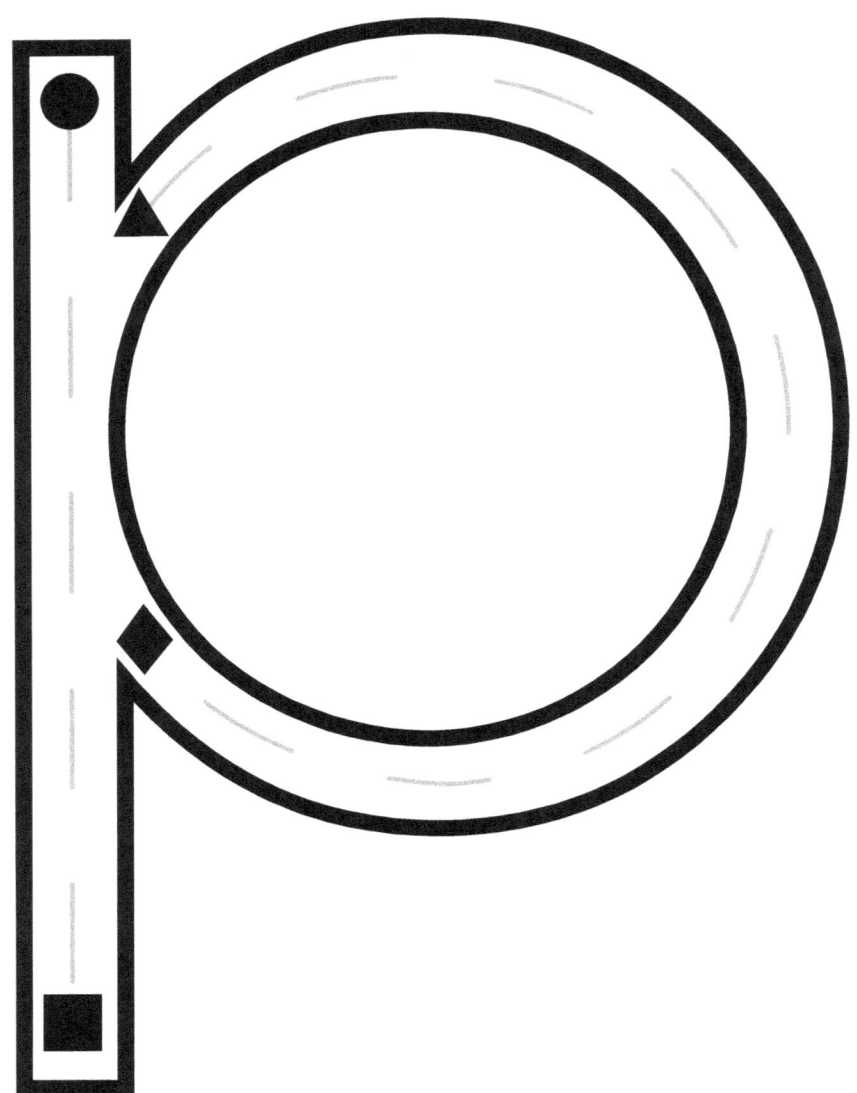

Practice tracing the lowercase p.

Now, trying writing a lowercase p on your own.

Color the picture.

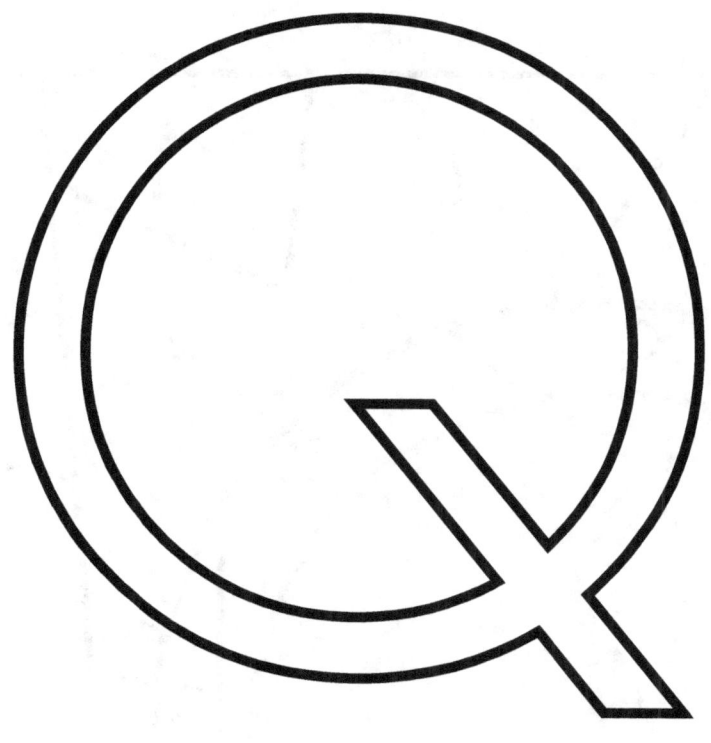

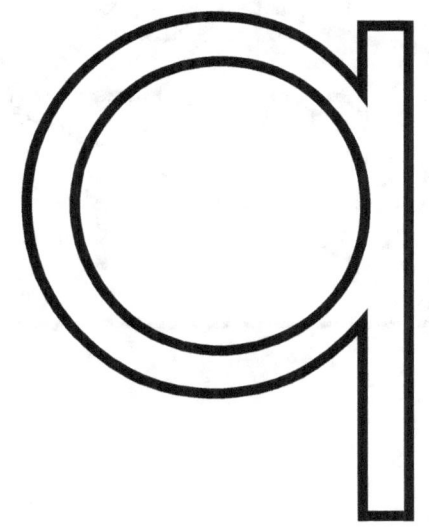

Learning ABC's Workbook: Print | Autumn McKay

Find the hidden picture by coloring all of the uppercase Q's and lowercase q's in the picture.

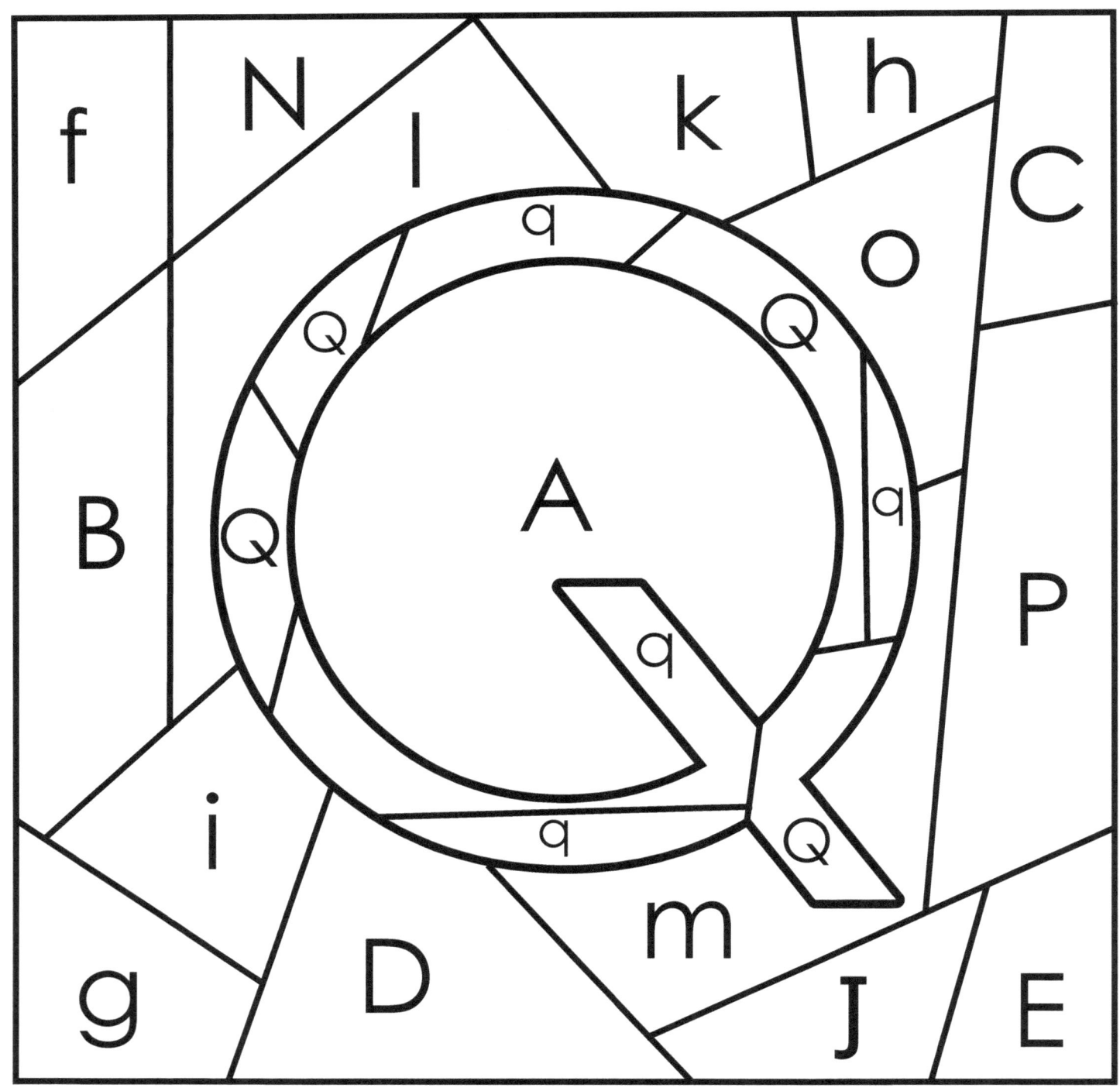

Start at the ●. Trace around to the ■. Place your pencil on the ▲. Trace down to the ♦.

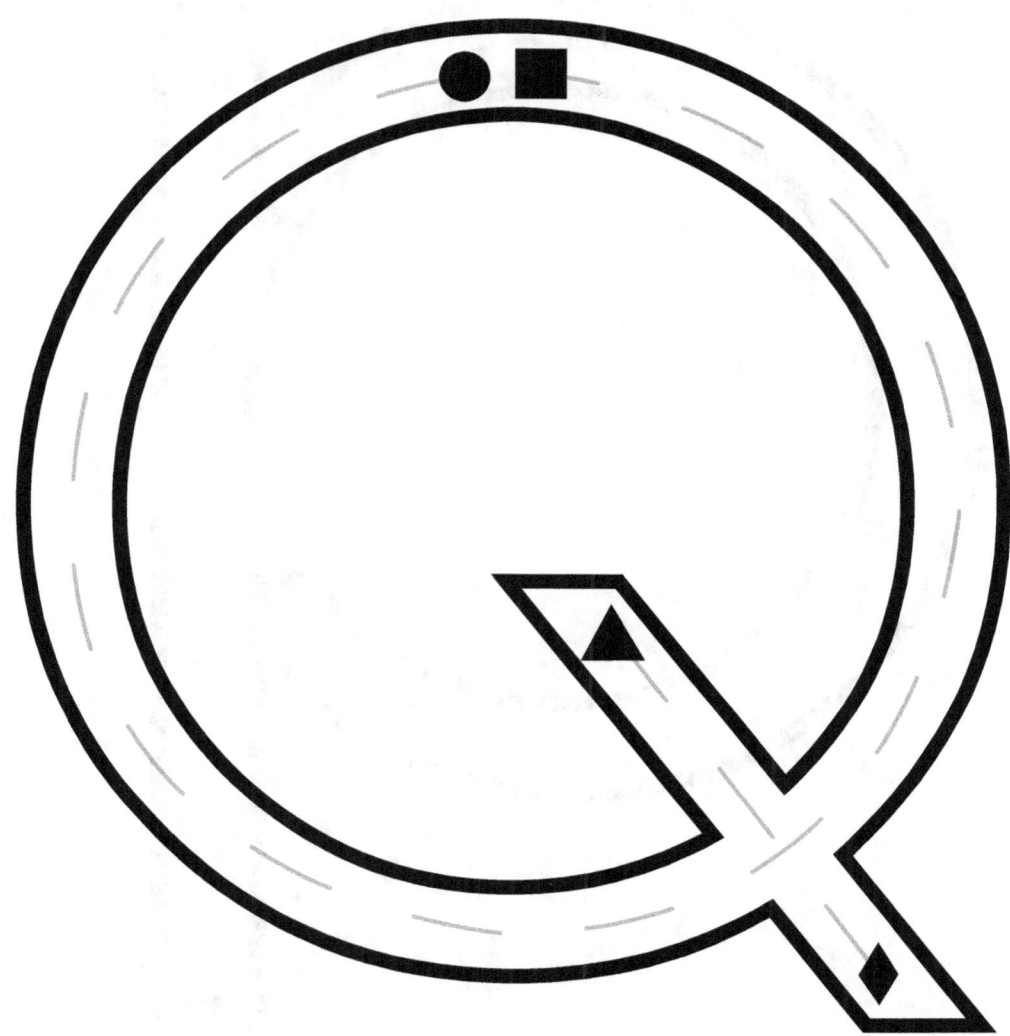

Practice tracing the uppercase Q.

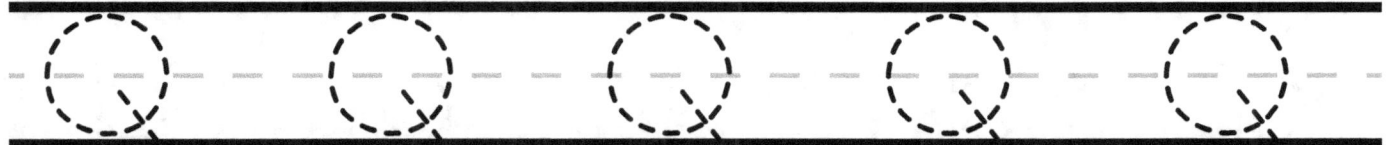

Now, try writing an uppercase Q on your own.

Start at the ●. Trace around to the ■. Place your pencil on the ▲, and trace down to the ♦.

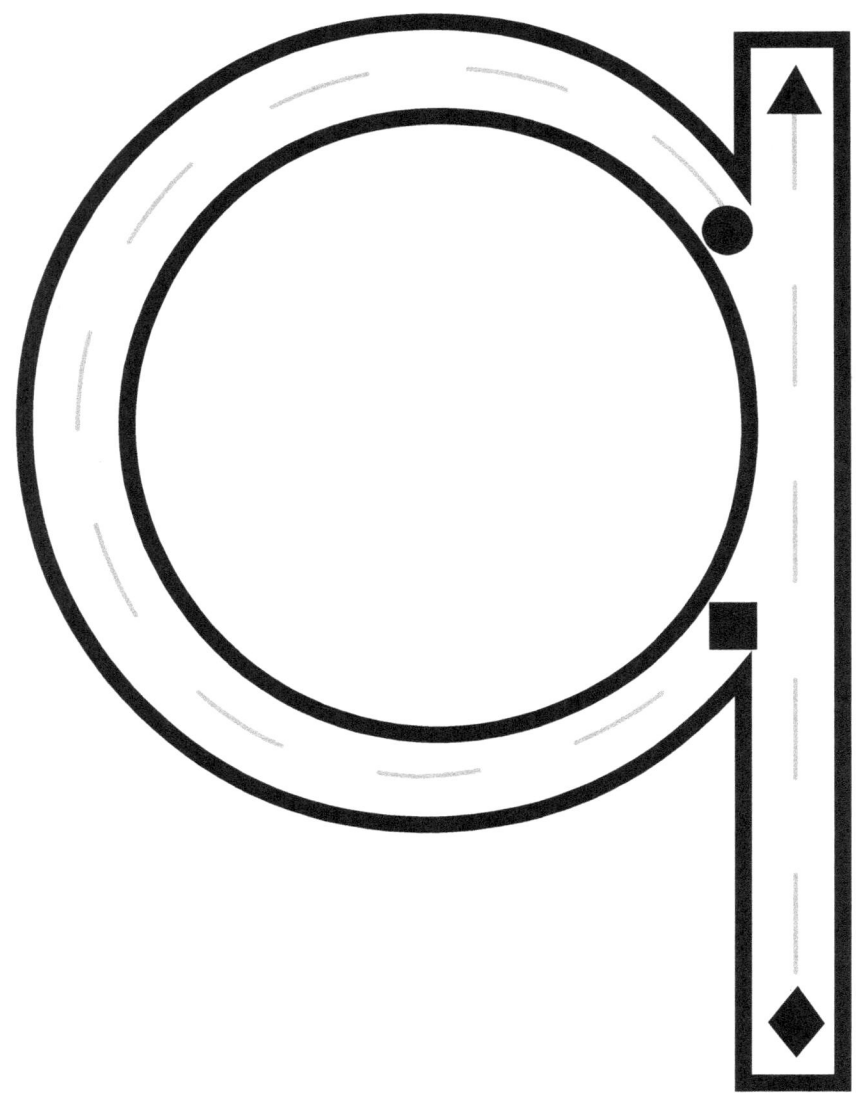

Practice tracing the lowercase q.

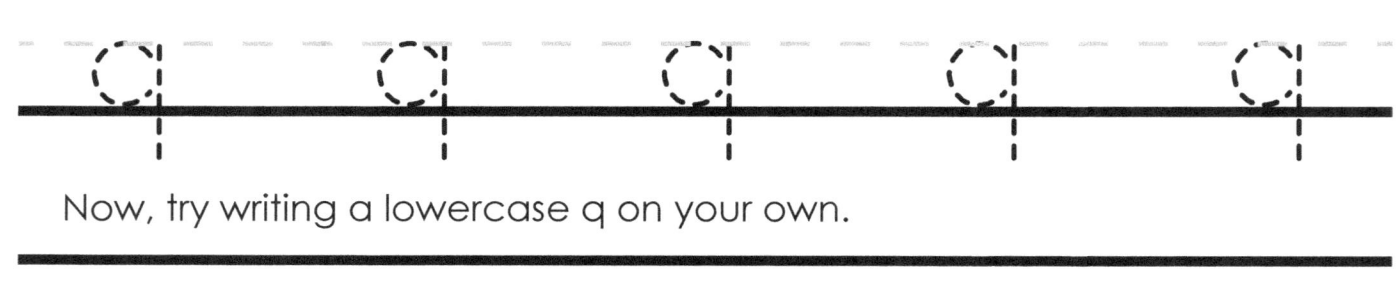

Now, try writing a lowercase q on your own.

Color the picture.

Color the uppercase R's orange. Color the lowercase r's purple.

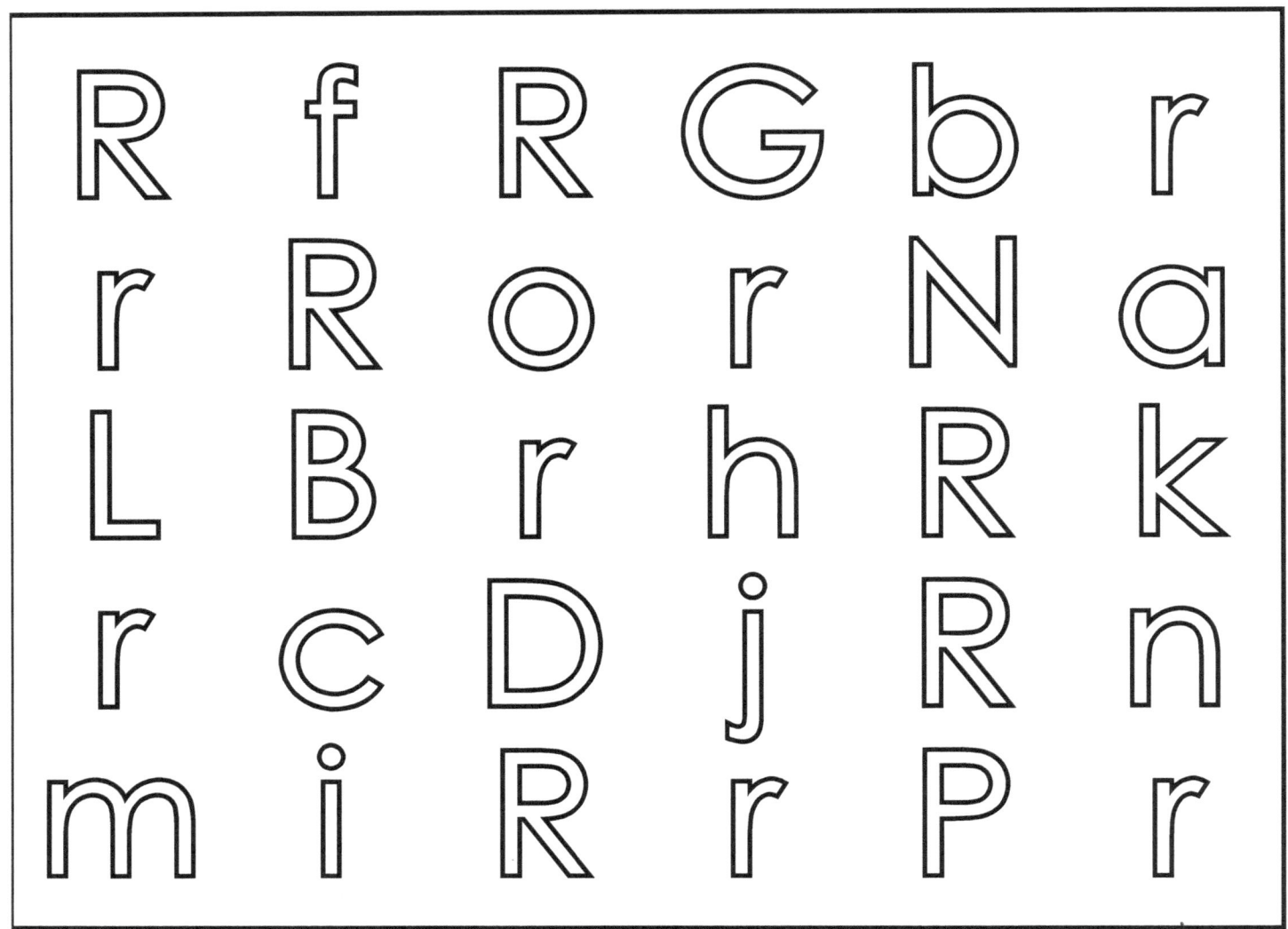

Place your pencil on the ●. Trace down to the ■. Place your pencil on the ▲, trace around to the ♦, and down to the ♥.

Practice tracing the uppercase R.

Now, try writing an uppercase R on your own.

Start at the ●. Trace down to the ■. Place your pencil on the ▲. Trace around to the ♦.

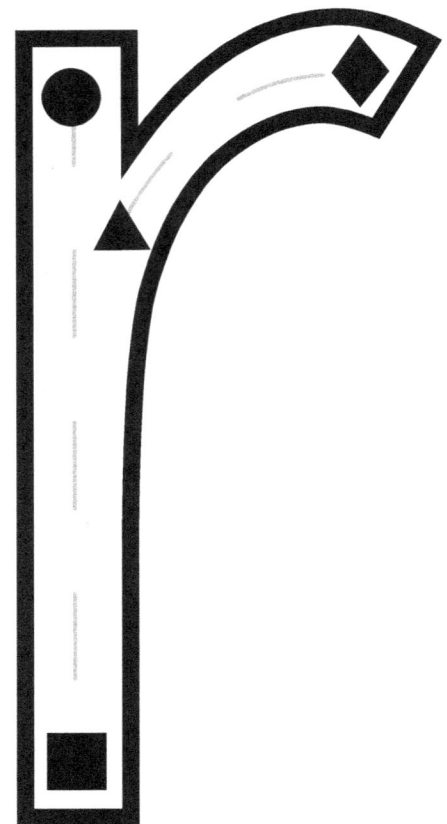

Practice tracing the lowercase r.

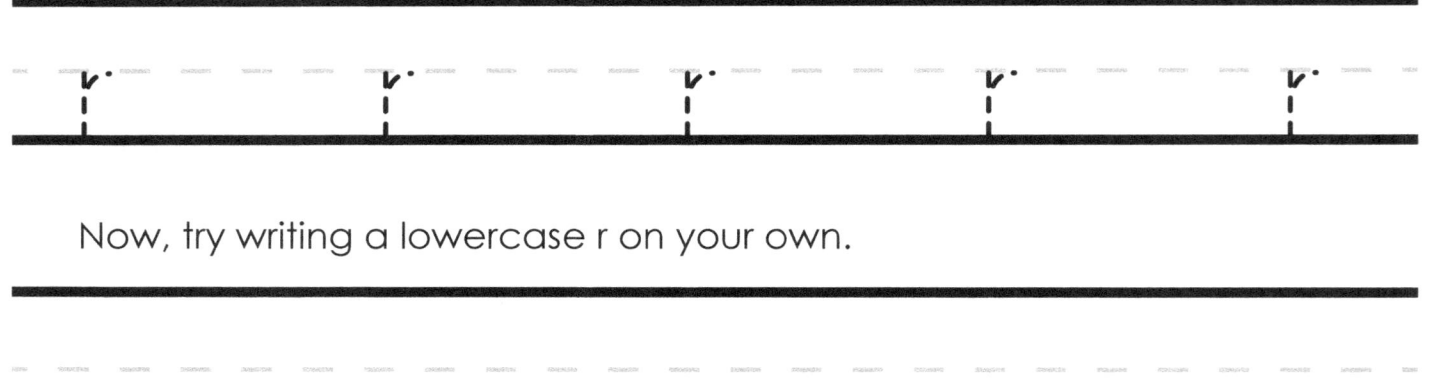

Now, try writing a lowercase r on your own.

Color the picture.

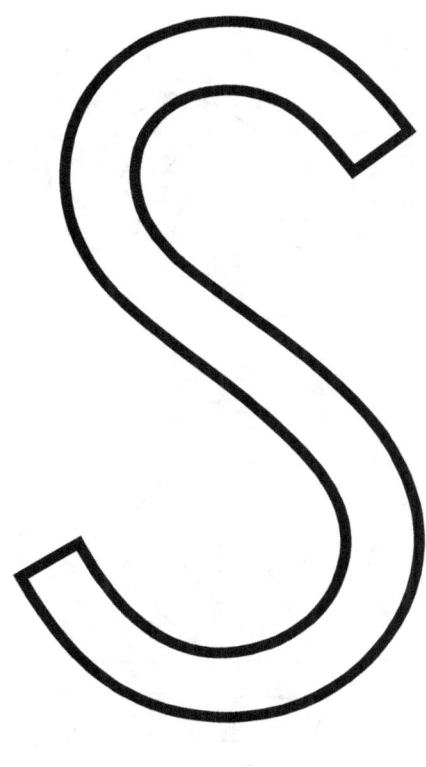

Circle the pictures that start with Ss.

Start at the ●. Trace the dotted line around and around to the ■.

Practice tracing the uppercase S.

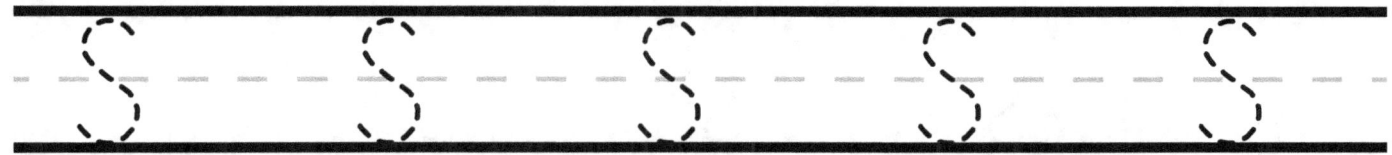

Now, try writing an uppercase S on your own.

Start at the ●. Trace the dotted line around and around to the ■.

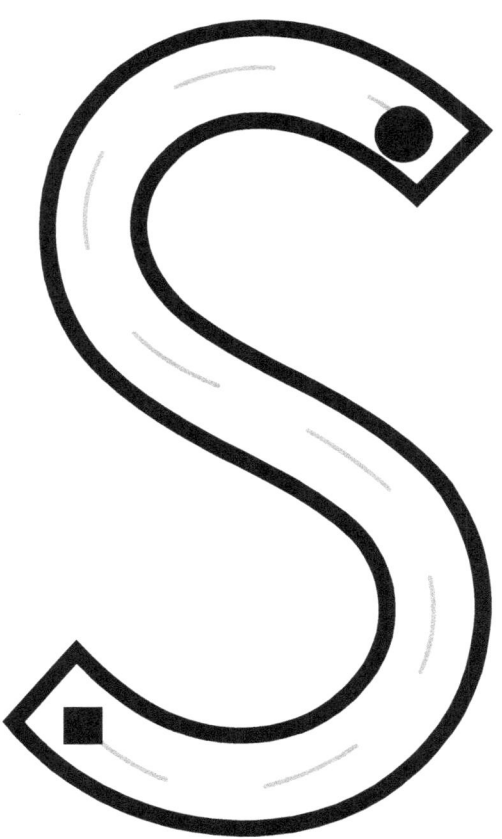

Practice tracing the lowercase s.

Now, try writing a lowercase s on your own.

Color the picture.

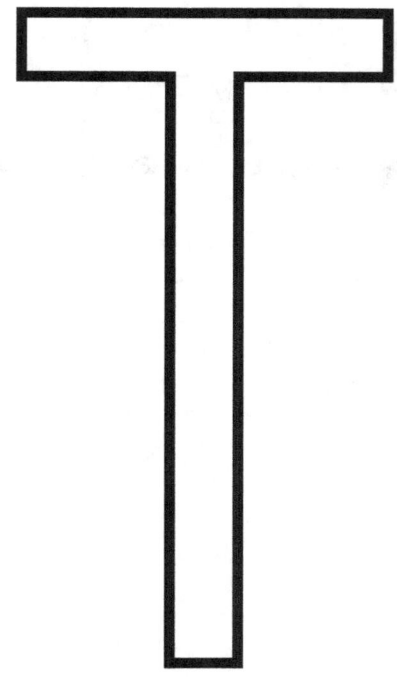

Help the **turtle** find his way through the maze to the **train**.

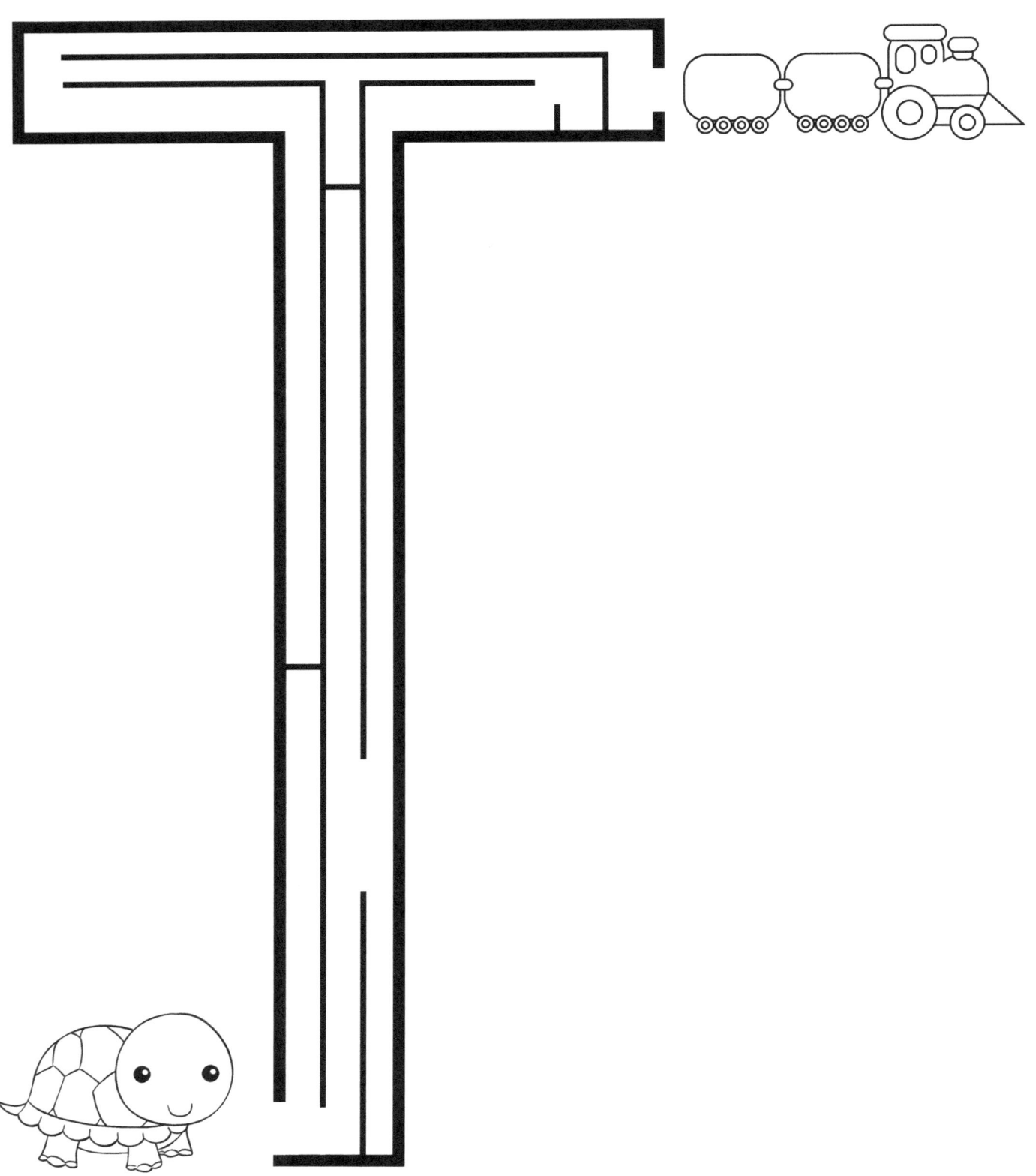

Start at the ●, and trace down to the ■. Place your pencil on the ▲, and trace across to the ♦.

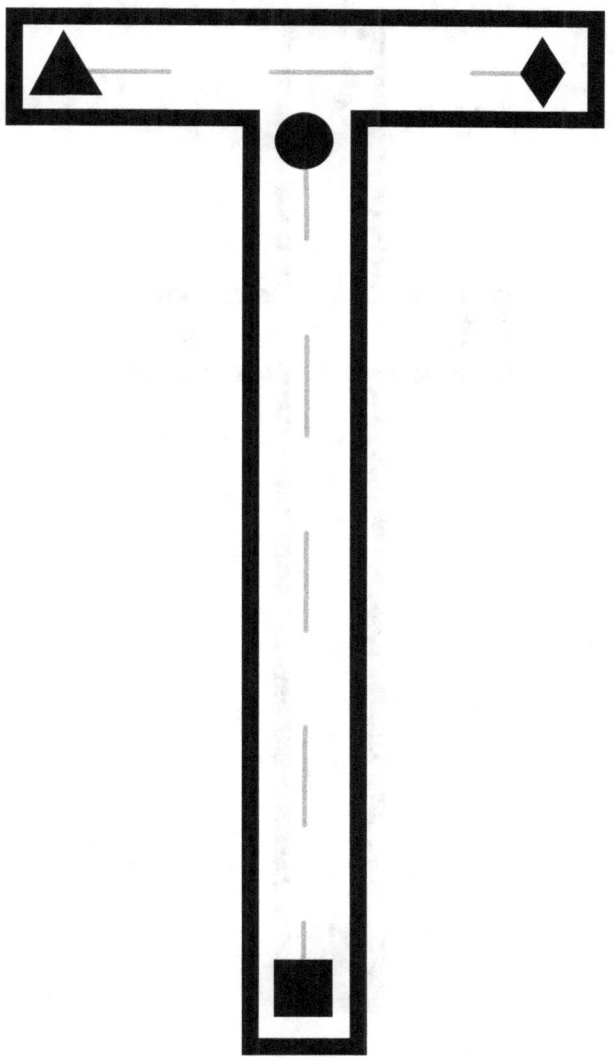

Practice tracing the uppercase T.

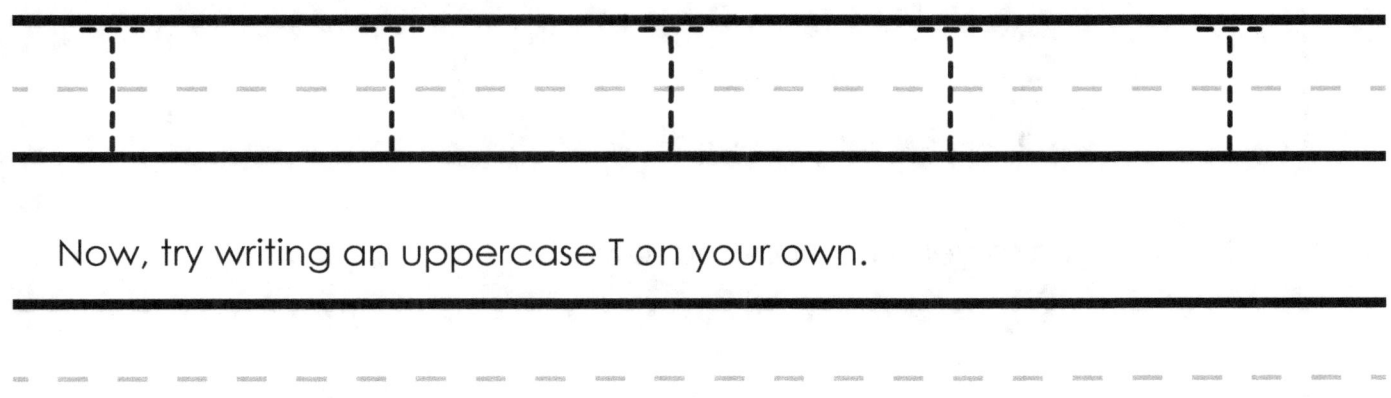

Now, try writing an uppercase T on your own.

Place your pencil on the ●. Trace down to the ■. Place your pencil on the ▲, and trace across to the ◆.

Practice tracing the lowercase t.

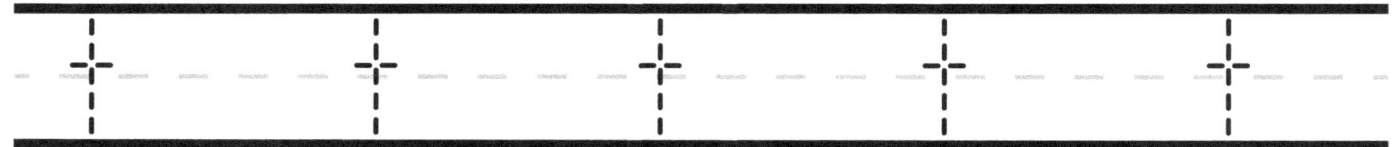

Now, try writing a lowercase t on your own.

Color the picture.

Place a sticker in each circle to form the letter U.

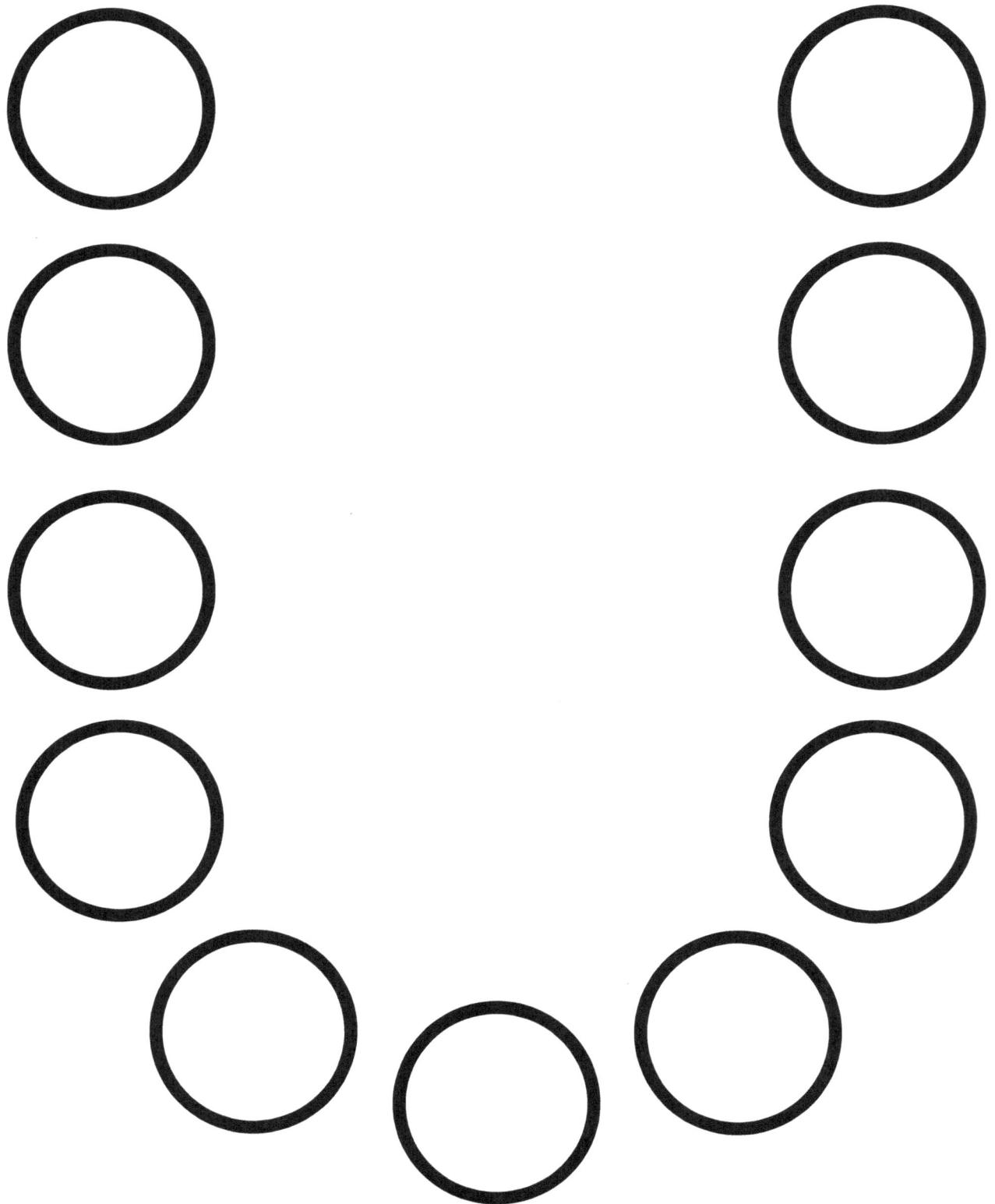

Start at the ●. Follow the dotted line around to the ■.

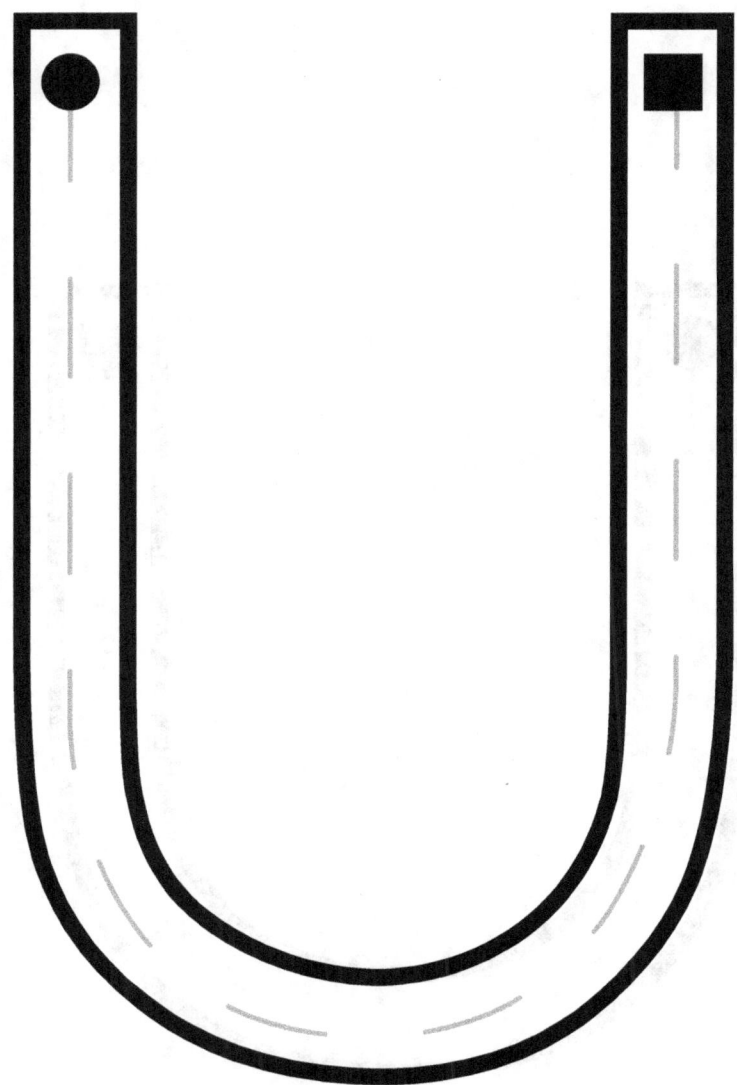

Practice tracing the uppercase U.

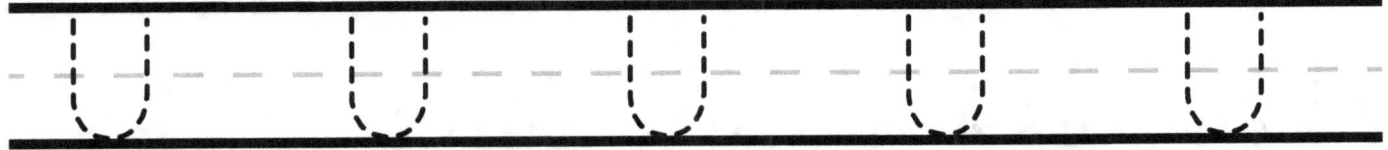

Now, try writing an uppercase U on your own.

Start at the ●. Follow the dotted line around to the ■.

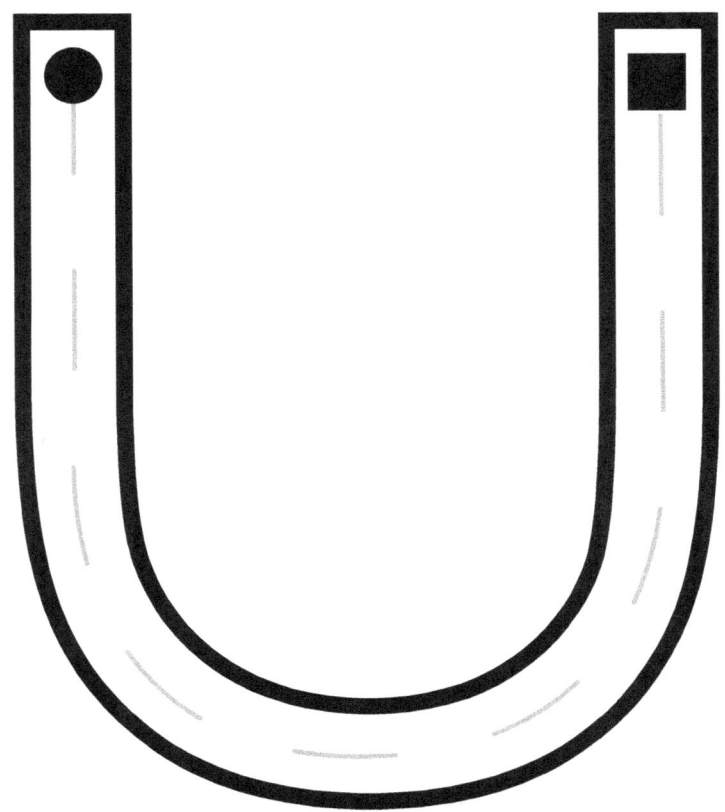

Practice tracing the lowercase u.

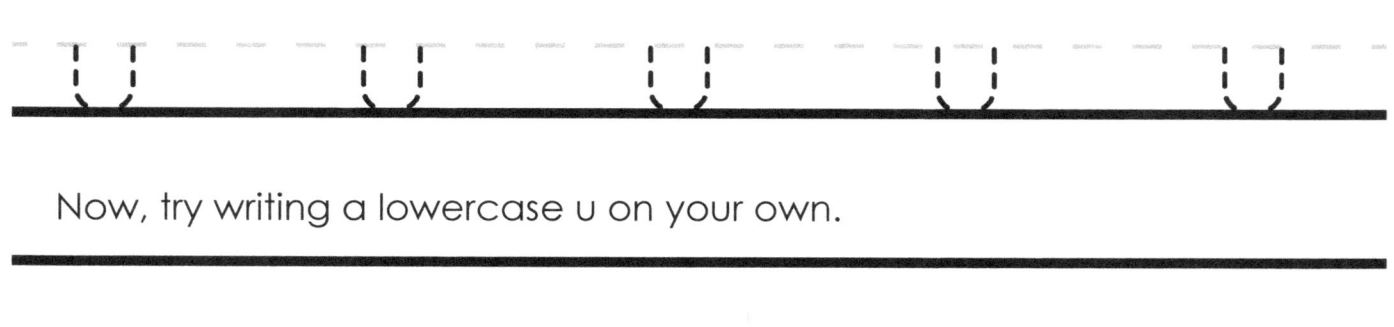

Now, try writing a lowercase u on your own.

Color the picture.

Left blank for cutting purposes.

Cut out the letter V.

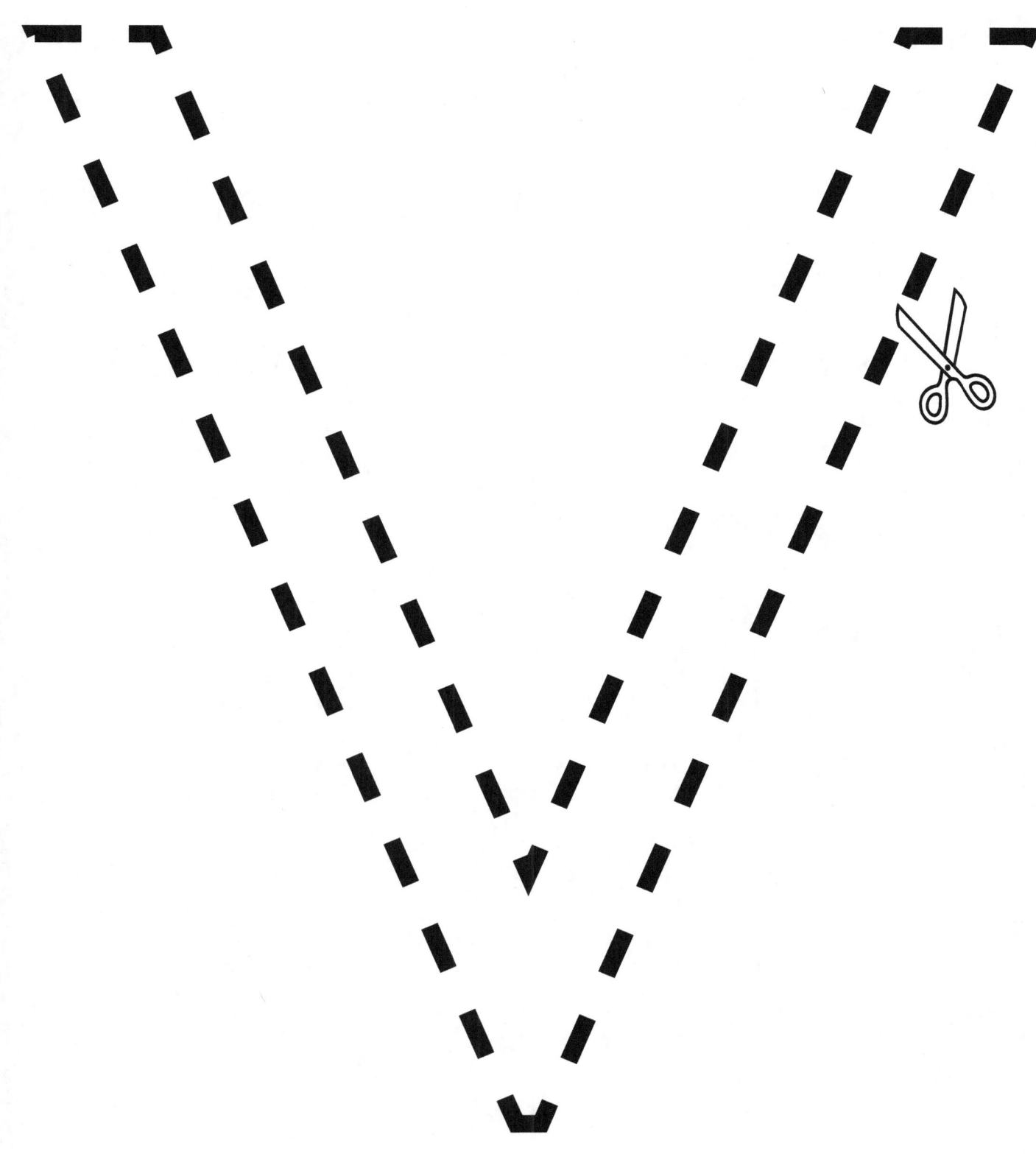

Place your pencil on the ●. Trace the dotted line down to the ■ and up to the ▲.

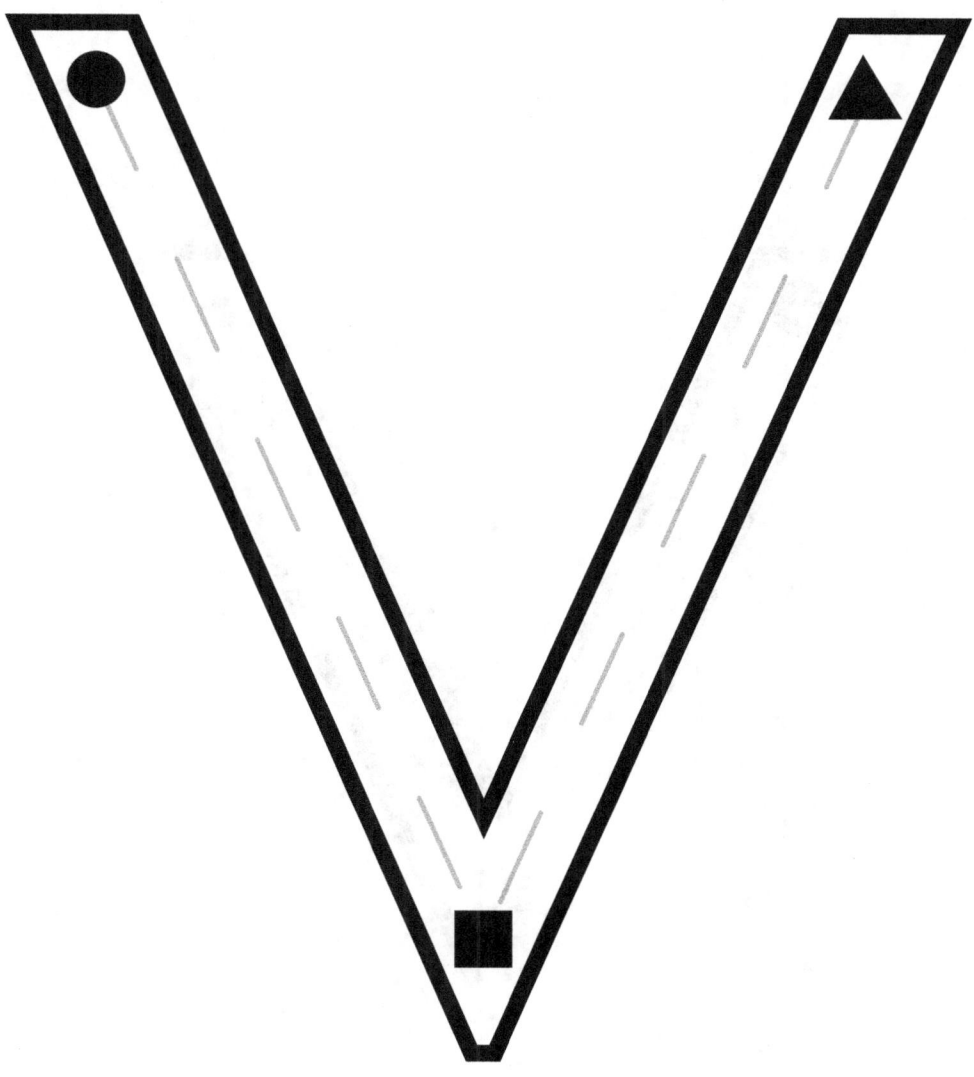

Practice tracing the uppercase V.

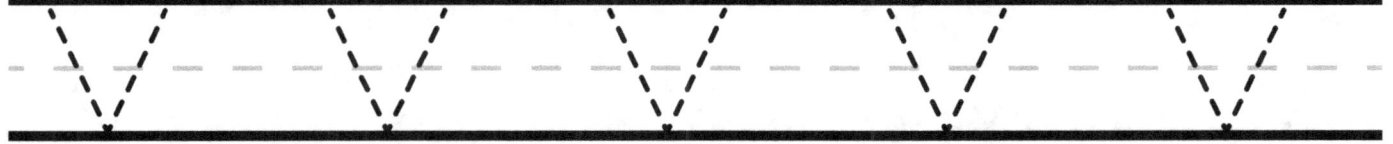

Now, try writing an uppercase V on your own.

Place your pencil on the ●. Trace the dotted line down to the ■ and up to the ▲.

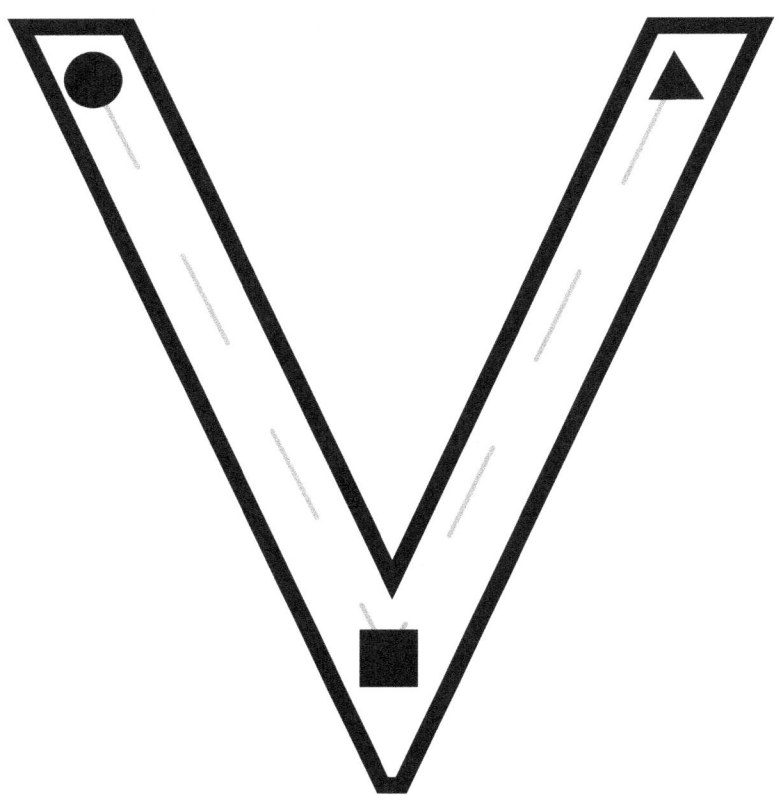

Practice tracing the lowercase v.

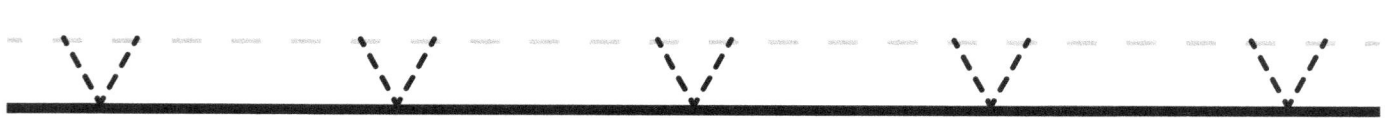

Now, try writing a lowercase v on your own.

Color the picture.

Circle the pictures that start with Ww.

Start at the ●. Trace the dotted line down to the ■, up to the ▲, down to the ♦, and up to the ♥.

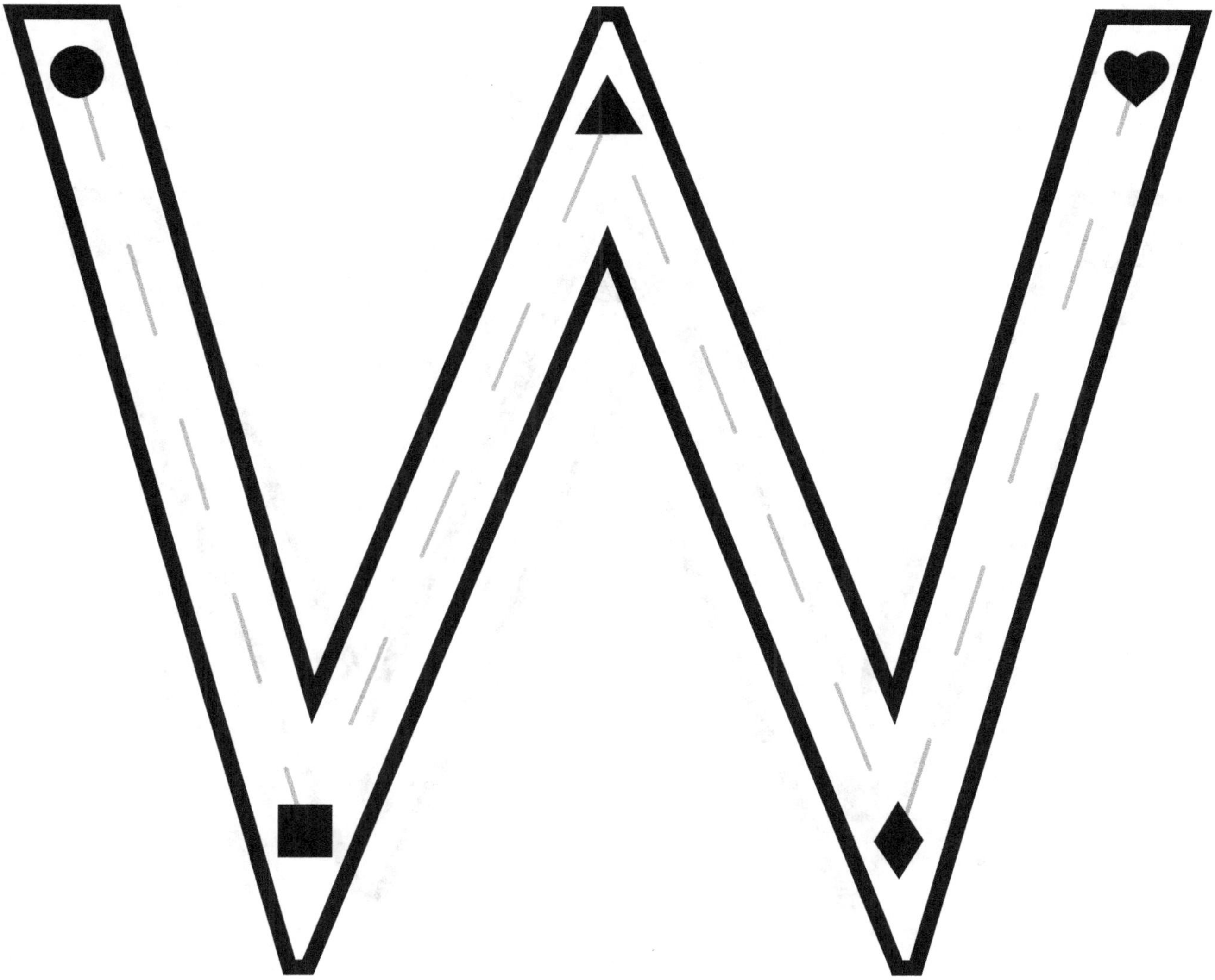

Practice tracing the uppercase W.

Now, try writing an uppercase W on your own.

Learning ABC's Workbook: Print | Autumn McKay

Start at the ●. Trace the dotted line down to the ■, up to the ▲, down to the ♦, and up to the ♥.

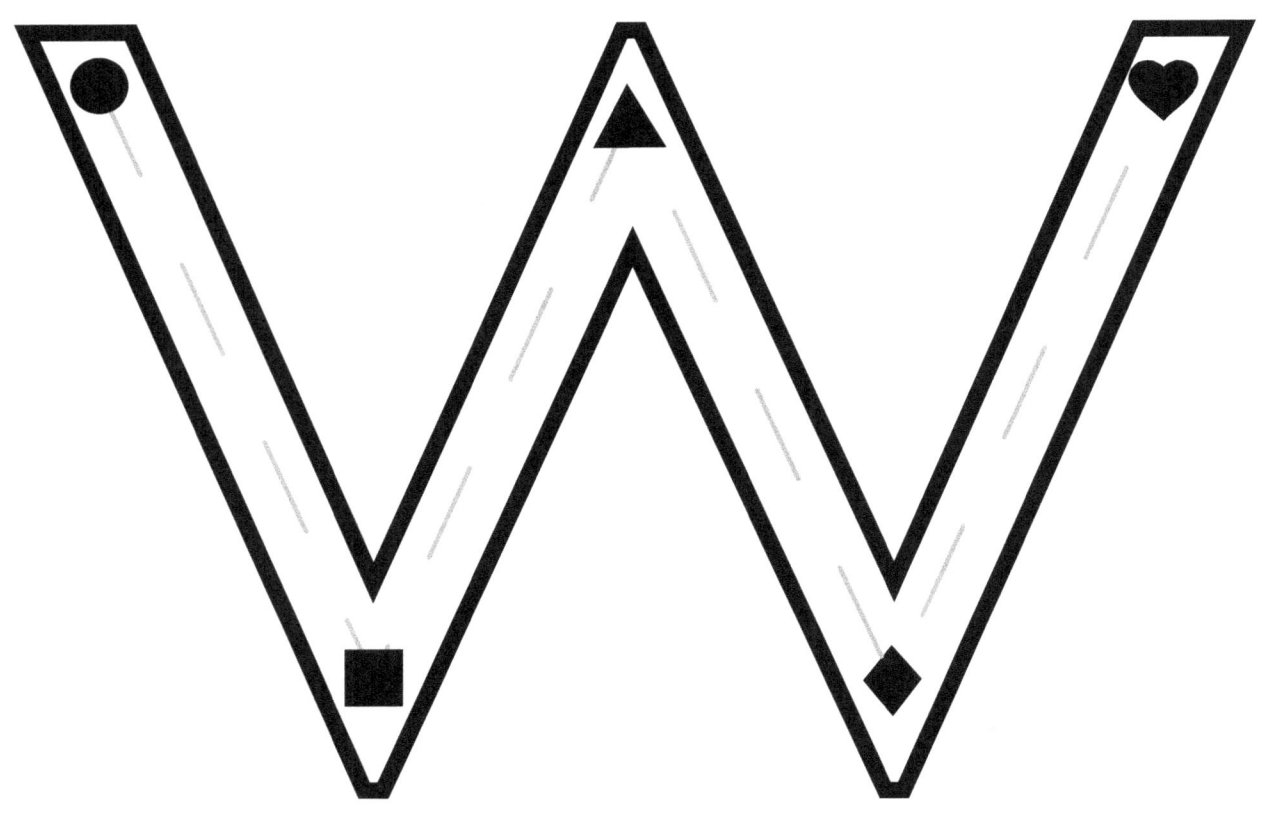

Practice tracing the lowercase w.

Now, try writing a lowercase w on your own.

Color the picture.

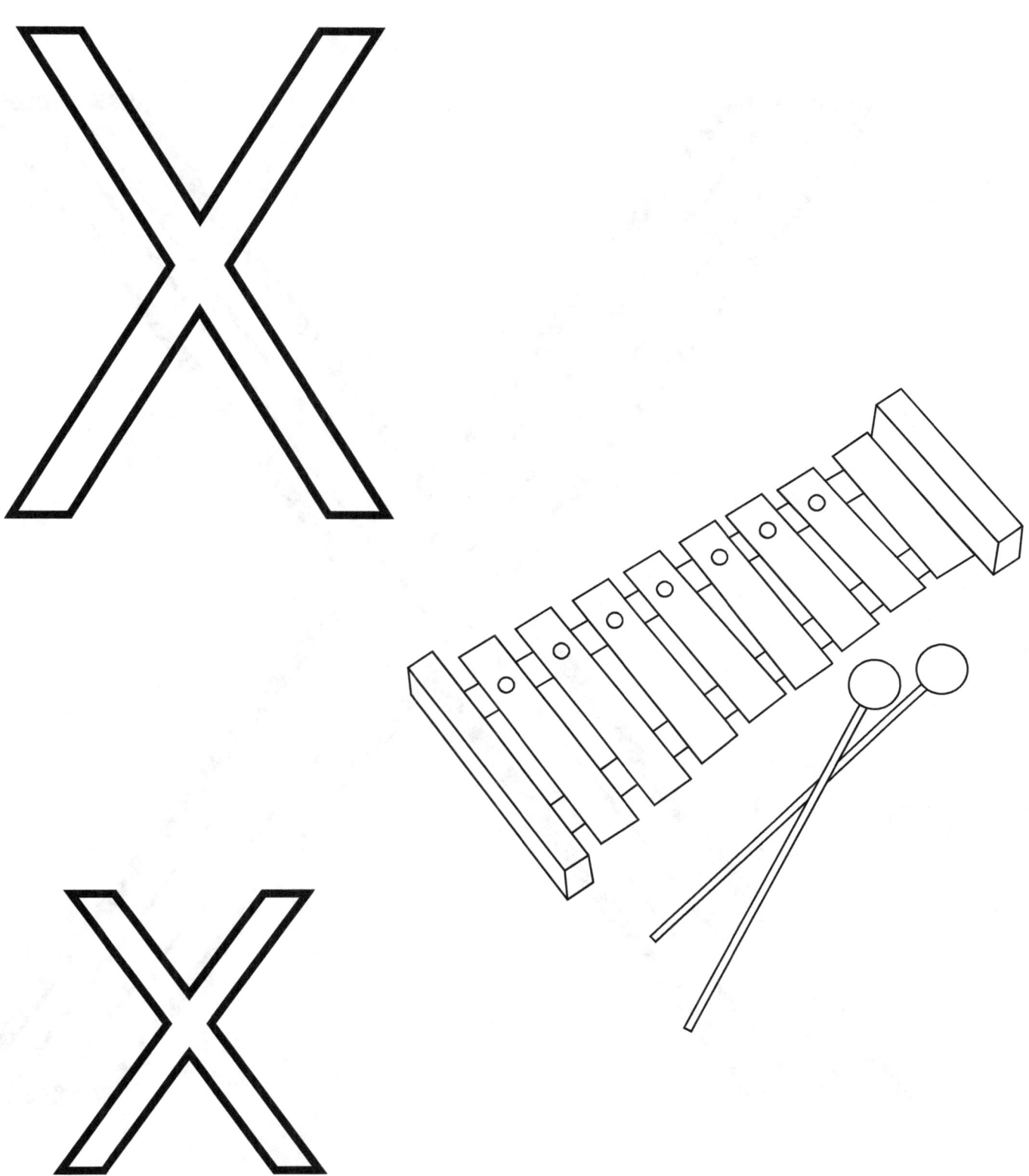

Help the **X-ray fish** find his way through the maze to the **x-ray machine.**

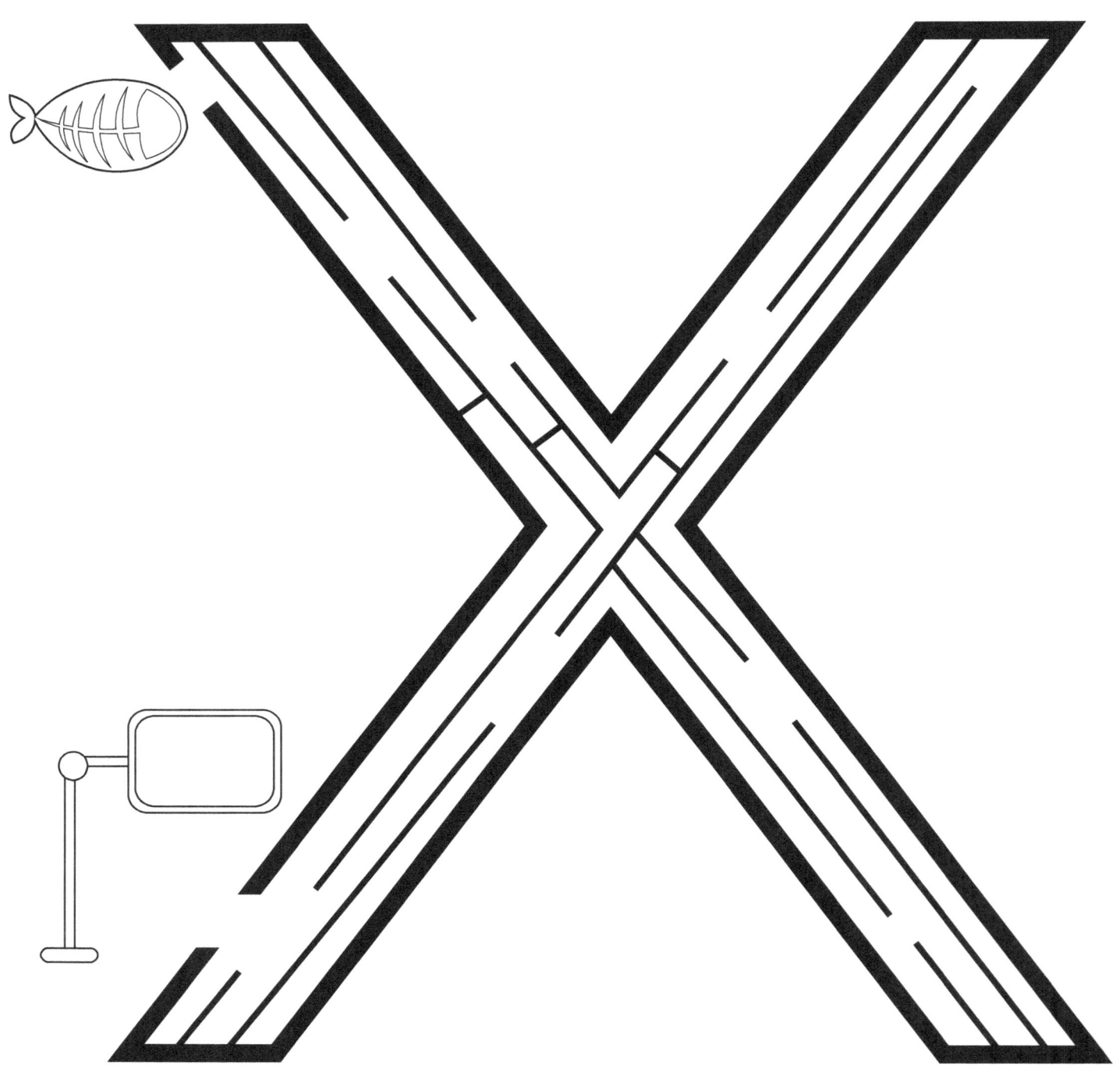

Start at the ●. Trace down to the ■. Place your pencil on the ▲, and trace down to the ♦.

Practice tracing the uppercase X.

Now, try writing an uppercase X on your own.

Start at the ●. Trace down to the ■. Place your pencil on the ▲, and trace down to the ♦.

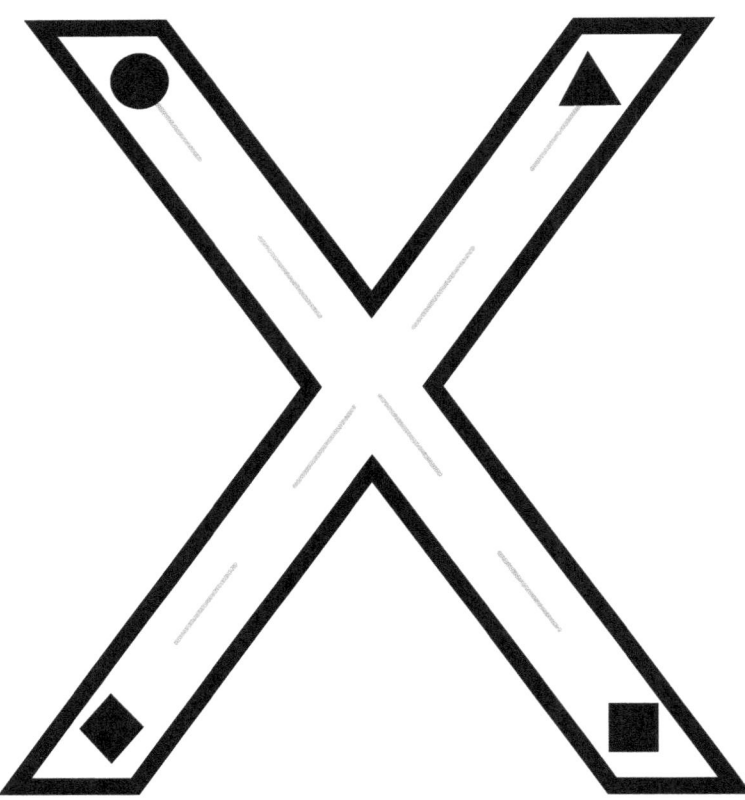

Practice tracing the lowercase x.

Now, try writing a lowercase x on your own.

Color the picture.

Y

y

Find the hidden picture by coloring all of the uppercase Y's and lowercase y's in the picture.

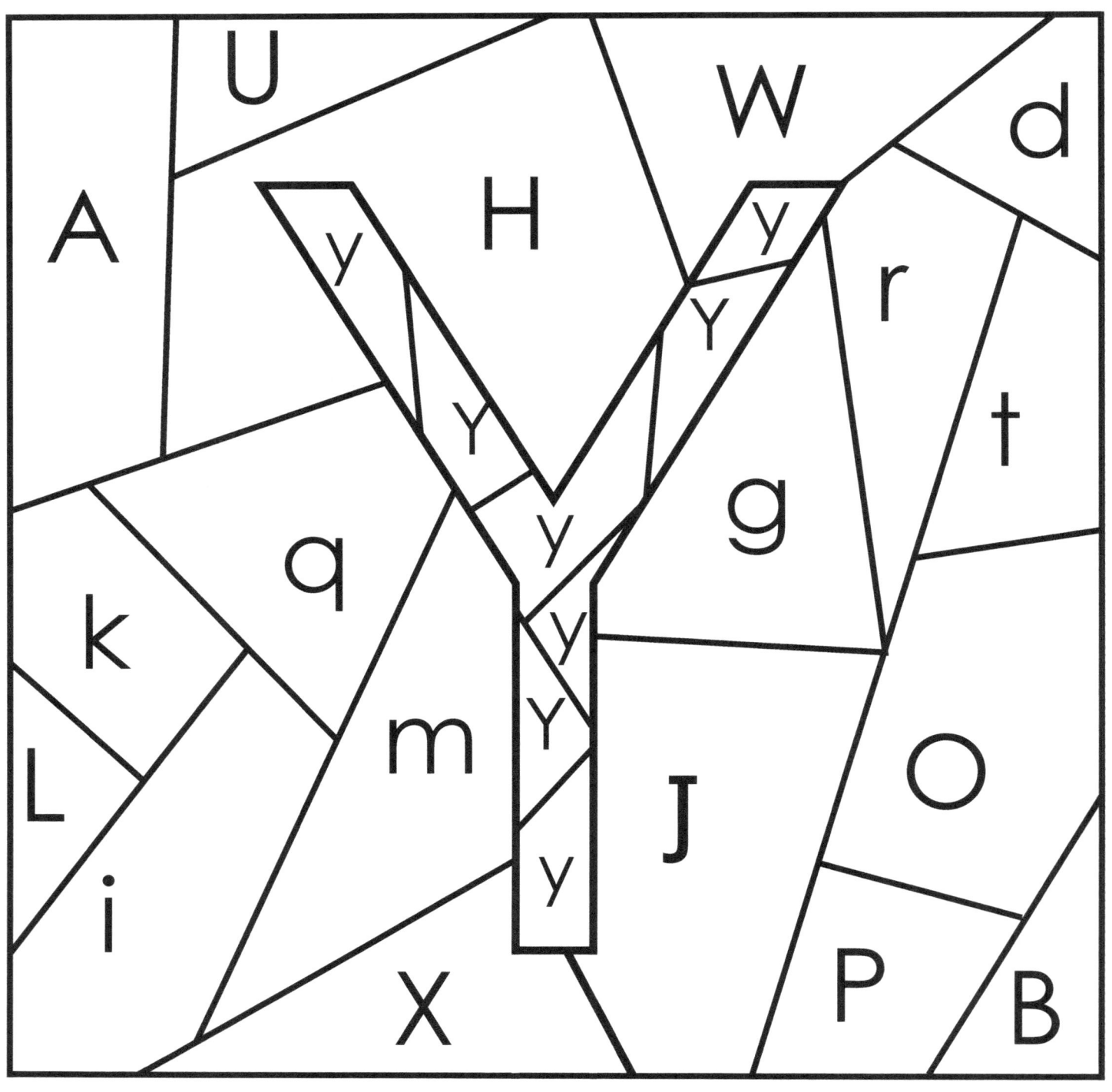

Start at the ●. Trace down to the ■. Place your pencil on the ▲. Trace down to the ◆.

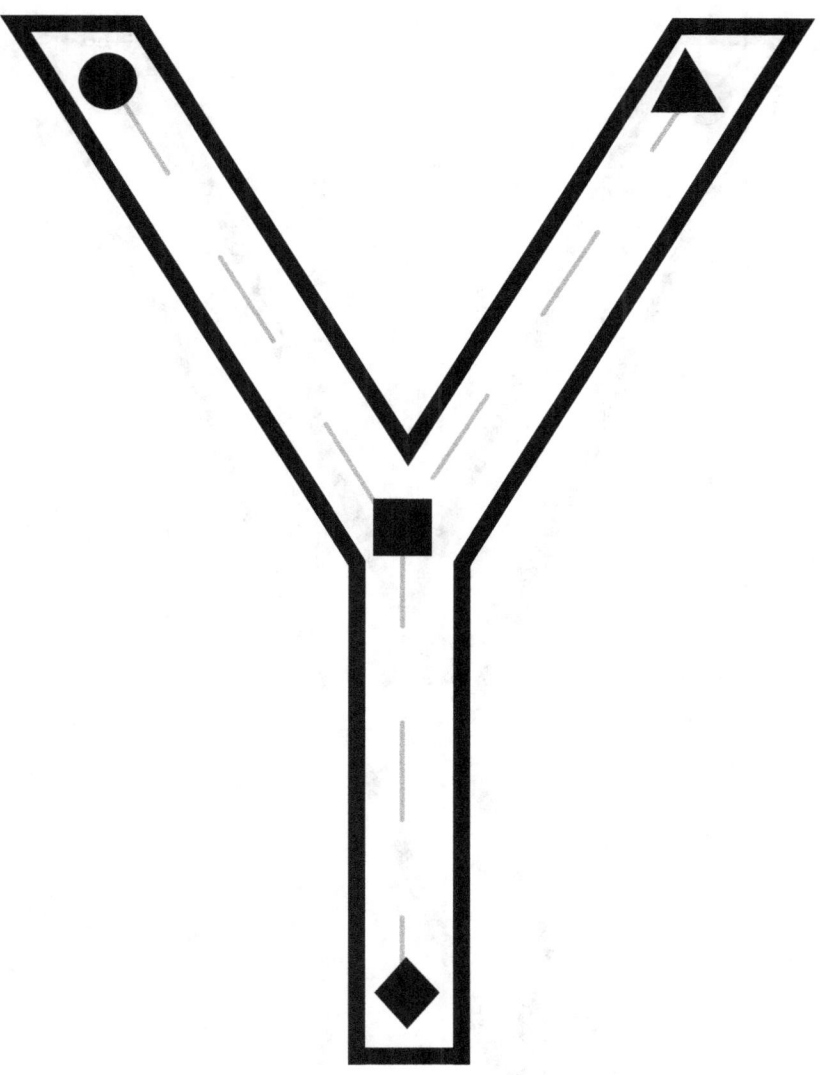

Practice tracing the uppercase Y.

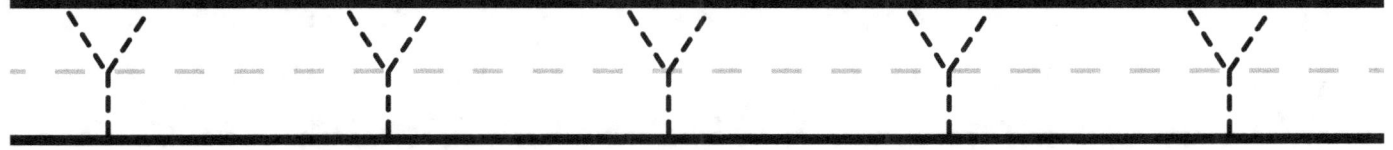

Now, trying writing an uppercase Y on your own.

Start at the ●. Trace down to the ■. Place your pencil on the ▲. Trace down to the ♦.

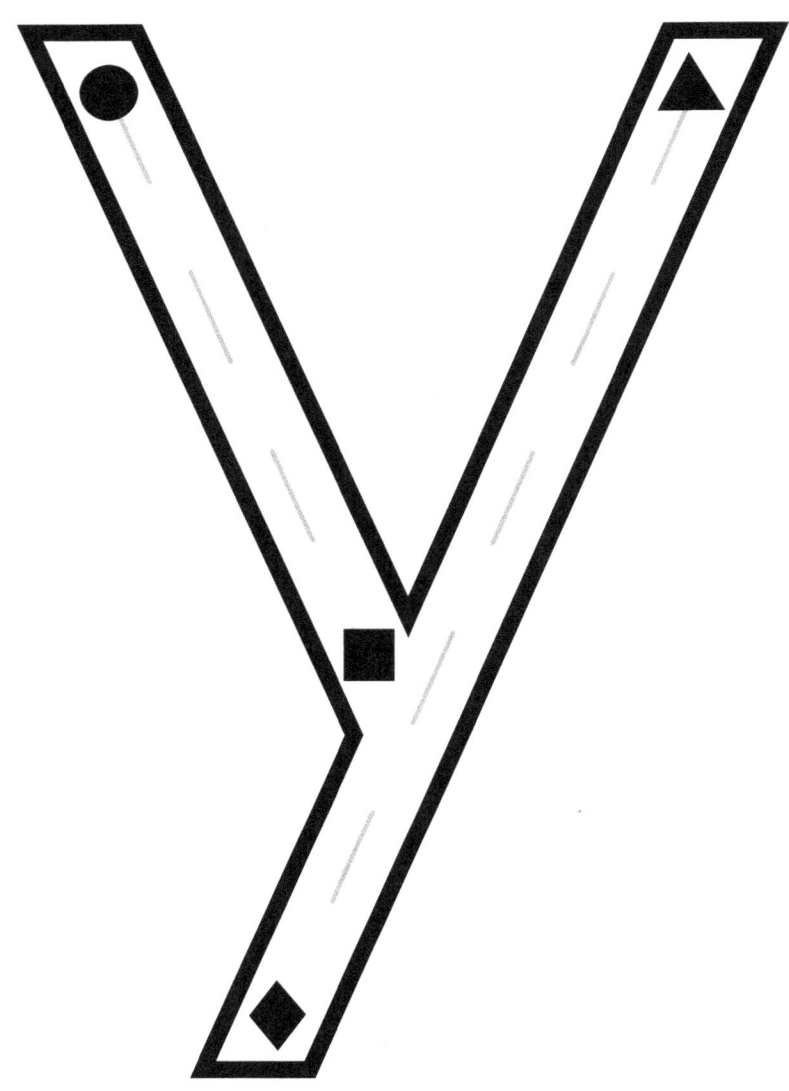

Practice tracing the lowercase y.

Now, trying writing a lowercase y on your own.

Color the picture.

Z

z

Color the uppercase Z's yellow. Color the lowercase z's pink.

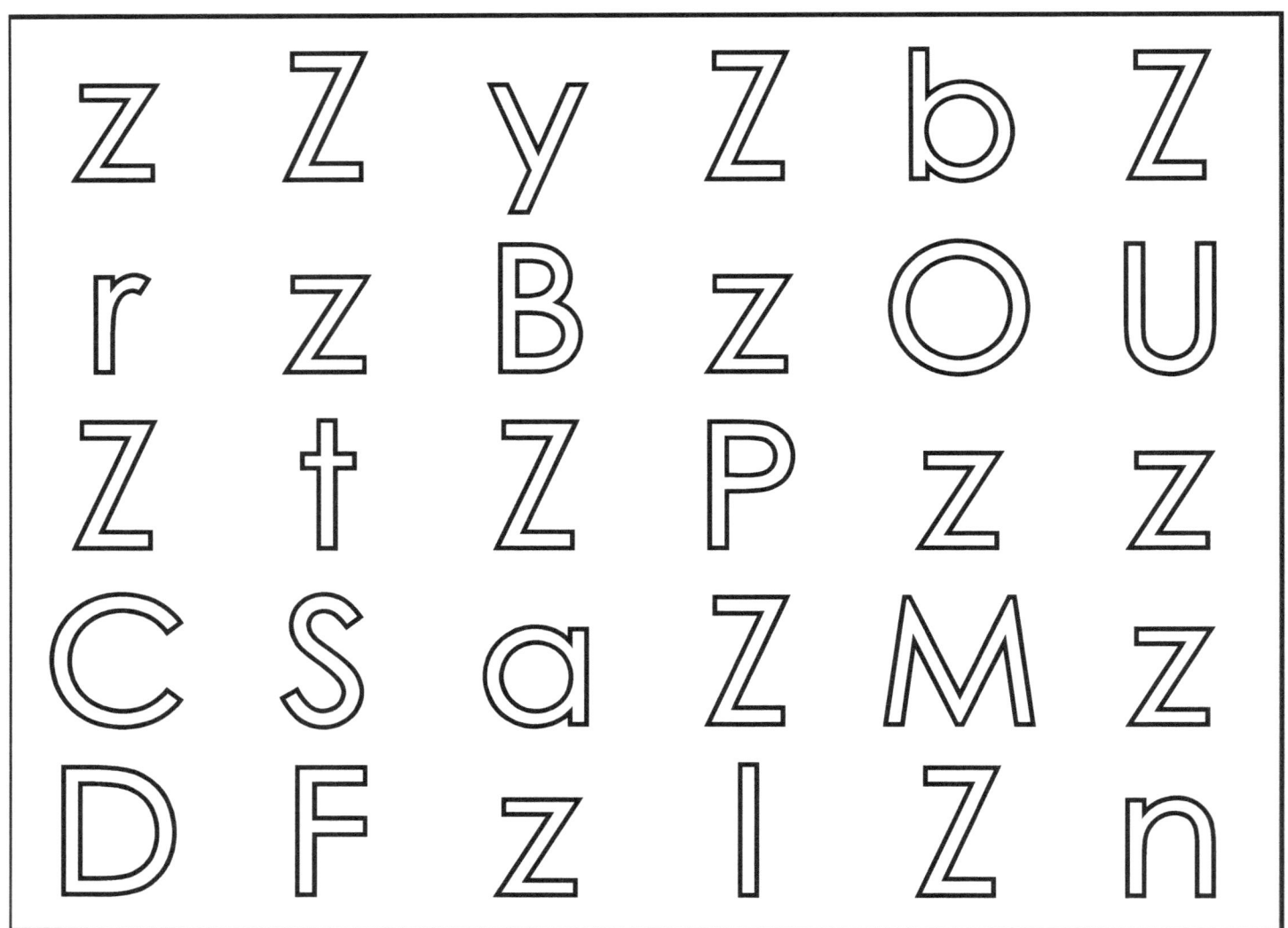

Start at the ●. Trace across to the ■, down to the ▲, and across to the ♦.

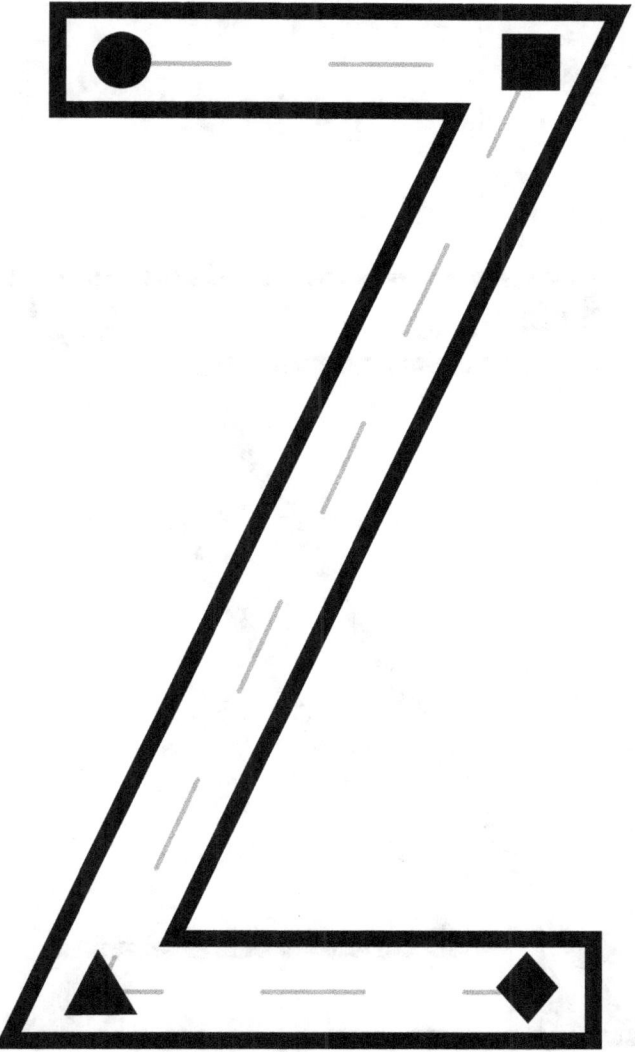

Practice tracing the uppercase Z.

Now, try writing an uppercase Z on your own.

Start at the ●. Trace across to the ■, down to the ▲, and across to the ◆.

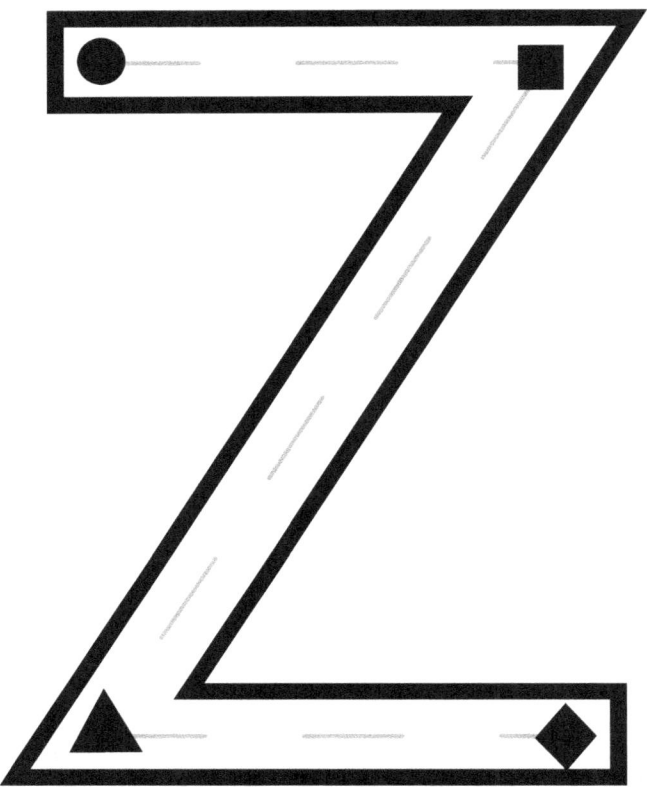

Practice tracing the lowercase z.

Now, try writing a lowercase z on your own.

Cut out the tiles on the next page. Sort all of the uppercase and lowercase letters into their correct column. Glue them in place.

Uppercase	Lowercase

Left blank for cutting purposes.

A	L	W	h	s
B	M	X	i	t
C	N	Y	j	u
D	O	Z	k	v
E	P	a	l	w
F	Q	b	m	x
G	R	c	n	y
H	S	d	o	z
I	T	e	p	
J	U	f	q	
K	V	g	r	

Learning ABC's Workbook: Print | Autumn McKay

Left blank for cutting purposes.

Congratulations!

You have successfully completed your Learning ABC's Workbook: Print!

Don't forget to claim your completion certificate. Scan the QR code or visit this link: www.bestmomideas.com/learning-abcs-print-certificate

Certificate of Completion

This Certifies That

_____

Has Successfully Trained & Completed the

LEARNING ABC'S WORKBOOK: PRINT

Parent/Guardian Signature: _____   Date: _____

Thank you for welcoming me into your home!
I hope you and your child liked learning together with this book!

If you enjoyed this book, it would mean so much to me
if you wrote a review so other moms can learn from your experience.

-♡- Autumn

Autumn@BestMomIdeas.com

Discover Autumn's Other Books

Early Learning Series

Early Learning Workbook Series

www.BestMomIdeas.com   @BestMomIdeas   Best Mom Ideas

www.ingramcontent.com/pod-product-compliance
Lightning Source LLC
Chambersburg PA
CBHW081750100526
44592CB00015B/2368